The Heart
Of The King

The Heart Of The King

THE QUEST BEGINS...

Donald Minter, General Editor

Columbus, Ohio

Contents

Editor's Note: The Google Effect

Several years ago, my middle son went to work for Google. I would soon learn firsthand what he and others meant when they said, "It's a Google world." While touring the campus just outside San Francisco, I began to understand the Google mantra repeated by those employed at the world's largest compiler of information, "You never want to leave!" With so many benefits for its employees, including continual free food, who would ever want to leave? Google was changing the world…

But Google's impact on the world is much more significant than how it treats its employees. Consider how we now acquire information, endless streams of data at our fingertips, all of it waiting for our beck and call. Want to do brain surgery? Just google it. Need to discover how to put together that new bicycle? Just google it. Google is now a verb that we all seem to understand: Seemingly endless accessible information waiting for your immediate application.

And there you have it, the key to how Google has changed the world: Immediate discovery and usage of information. Memorization a thing of the past. Just google it. And the world will never be same.

I often suggest the key to a thriving devotional life is the google effect: immediate application. Or, as the old saying goes, "Use it, or lose it." Welcome to the world of Google. Life will never be the same.

If you have this book, you are part of a small community, a gathering of folks who meet in the world of Google, Facebook, Vimeo, Instagram, and all the rest. Each morning, our media team will post a daily two-minute video and transcript (FlagNaz Daily Briefing on Facebook), as we systematically chase after the Serving King in the Gospel of Matthew. We invite you to join the conversation.

But rest assured, without the google effect, immediate application, you will soon fatigue of the daily gathering. We hope you will join us, as we love on in the way of the Serving King…

Contributing Authors:

Donald Minter
Brian Spencer
Melissa Rightmire
Charles Christian
Melodie Eisenhofer
John Letterman
Doug Ward
Bob Hunter
Jeffrey Paparone
Stephanie Boardman
Blake Boardman
Rachel Shald
Tim Masters
Randy Green
Duane Sonneberg
David Charlton
Will Hathaway
Steve VanDalen
Dan Schafer
Pam Golliet
Mindy States
Daniel Rogers
Ali Gentry
Sarah Crouch
Vincent Carotenuto
Katie Donaldson
Ryan Albaugh

General Editor

Donald Minter
Laura Minter

DAY 1

DNA Matters

"If you accept the belief that baptism incorporates us in the mystical body of Christ, into the divine DNA, then you might say that the Holy Spirit is present in each of us, and thus we have the capacity for the fullness of redemption, of transformation." —Thomas Keating

The book of the genealogy of Jesus Christ, the Son of David, the Son of Abraham.
(Matthew 1:1)

Unlike John, writer or the Gospel of the same name, Matthew links the genealogy of Jesus to His earthly ancestors, those profoundly human folk, damaged and tainted just like the rest of us. For those early readers, the intention was clear: He is one of us, more like us than we sometimes like to admit. So begins our journey into Matthew.

It was perhaps the strangest birthday present I have ever seen. Nonetheless, there it was, a DNA kit for my wife, a cherished gift from a close friend. And Laura was beyond excited. Like so many in the modern era, my bride was anxious to learn everything she could about her ancestors, more to the point, the propensities they have passed onto her. Knowing them, their very DNA, helped her to understand how and why she operates the way she does. Her genealogy provides an incredible amount of insight into who she is.

Matthew had similar thoughts as he introduced folks to the Serving King, the Messiah, Jesus the Christ. Specifically, in what ways is Jesus like us, and to what extent can He save us, redeem us from our brokenness? Perhaps, His DNA helps Him to understand us, really grasp what we are up against as we battle the raging flesh relentlessly pursing us, attempting to drag us into the worst versions of who we can be.

For Matthew, the lineage links two giants of the faith: Abraham and David. Like the rest of us, these two giants rise up out of the brokenness of the human condition, warts and all. And yes, the lineage Jesus embraces provides Him with a keen insight into the battles you and I face. But unlike Abraham and David, Jesus will conquer the flesh, providing hope and encouragement for all who decide to trek after the Serving King. So begins our journey into the life of Jesus, following closely on His heels, learning what only He can teach us as we trek on after the Serving King. The challenge to keep loving is just beginning...
DM

Embracing The Mundane

We are enmeshed in a lineage that came from somewhere and is going to make way for the next generation." —Leon Kass

Abraham was the father of Isaac, and Isaac the father of Jacob, and Jacob the father of Judah and... (Matthew 1:2-5)

In our quest to be like the Serving King, we are often tempted to transform Him into something outside Jewish traditions, above the Law as it were. As the Son of God, born by virgin birth, He must be something wholly other than anything that came before. We wish this were true, desiring a pathway leading us out of our human condition into something beyond the Law, external to the modern culture where being like Jesus comes naturally.

Matthew allows no such reveling in this mirage, even for a moment. Immediately, he makes clear the story we are about to read is fundamentally Jewish. All Israelites trace their ancestry to Abraham, the ultimate patriarch. They know their tribe. They know their fathers – all of them. Jesus is no different, a son of Abraham from the tribe of Judah. There is no exemption from being one of them. Jesus is an Israelite bound to the Law of Moses.

This particular genealogy is more interesting than most. Matthew slyly suggests one of the most famous prostitutes ever is one of Jesus' mothers. He then continues with a Moabitess, a foreigner, a widow, someone marginalized and disregarded by society. The Son of God was not exempted from being one of them, He came from notorious stock, determined to overcome what others could not.

The temptation to believe we will follow the Serving King out of our story and into an untarnished one is dashed to pieces. Instead, it dawns on us the amazing will occur in the midst of broken normality. The sublime will be revealed within the mundane. God is the missing ingredient turning a haphazard lineage of the ordinary and misfits into priceless royalty. The inherent incompleteness of our heart is not a flaw; it is an open window, waiting for Him. It is here, at the beginning of His story, that we start to desire the unimaginable, the ability to love like a servant in our present conditions. Keep loving...

BS

A Long Line Of Glorious Failure

"Success is the result of perfection, hard work, learning from failure, loyalty, and persistence." —Colin Powell

And David was the father of Solomon by the wife of Uriah, Solomon the father of Rehoboam, and... (Matthew 1:7-11)

As we moderns receive the lengthy list of the Serving King's ancestors, we tend to gloss over the names, swiftly moving ahead to the point where the real story begins. Our minds are bored, eager to be engaged. More insidiously, our hearts seek to avoid this introduction, intuitively knowing there is meaning under the surface. Skimming along, our eyes and minds may miss the texture but our hearts do not. They are instead repulsed, desperate for the happy ending. Those insistent upon learning to love like a servant will do the hard work here, knowing God must reveal truth – ours and His – before we can be who He would have us to be.

Pleased at possibly avoiding the painful reminder of our incompleteness, our willingness to be of the world, we read that David – King David – is one of Jesus' fathers. This reminds us of the unfailing faithfulness of God, having fulfilled His covenant with David of an eternal kingdom. Then Matthew reminds us that David fell as far as any into sin and despair; from a man after God's own heart to sluggard, adulterer, and murderer. God could have swept this aside, bringing Jesus forth through another of David's sons. Instead, God is a redeemer and restorer, a transformer. He illuminates the truth of David, as He prepares to bring forth His Truth, the Light of the world.

So it goes, each name significant in the history of Israel, a history about to be forever altered by God's intercession in the life of His people. Our hearts are pierced by the necessity to face our truth, to stand bare before the mirror and acknowledge our historic reality. This is no timid glance. Only once our spiritual history is unpacked and inspected can we approach the Healer, who knows just where we hurt and need His touch. Touch us, He will, forever altering our historic future as He readies us to love others as only He can. Do the hard work so one day you too can love like the Serving King. Keep loving...

BS

DAY 4

Deportation

"It all happened so fast. The ghetto. The deportation. The sealed cattle car. The fiery altar upon which the history of our people and the future of mankind were meant to be sacrificed." —Elie Wiesel

And after the deportation to Babylon: Jechoniah was the father of Shealtiel, and Shealtiel the father of Zerubbabel... (Matthew 1:12-16)

Matthew glances over it without even pausing, just another piece of the mundane, a subtle reminder of the extreme conditions often unfolding in the journey of God's people. Entire books of the Old Testament are dedicated to the tale, glorious tales of adventure, miraculous interventions in the lives of God's people. They, too, in the moment of 'deportation', were tempted to think the trek after the Serving King must be drawing to a close, a final chapter in the meanderings of God's people. But there is no final chapter in the trek after the Serving King; instead, only moments of 'deportation', pauses in the quest, detours on the journey toward final significance.

In your moment of 'deportation', and, yes, we all have them in one fashion or another, you will be tempted to lament, allowing despair to crash over your existence, thinking your moment of 'deportation' a final chapter in your personal quest to stay on the heels of the Serving King. But your quest is not over, nor is this your final destination. Like all who have trekked after the Serving King, this is but a layover, a mere moment in the journey away from the comforts of home. There are still many chapters to discover in the tale ahead.

But there will come a time in the years ahead when your children's children will tell the tale of your 'deportation', glancing quickly over the details, just an allusion to another step in the journey that brought them to their own present moment. Your moment of 'deportation' is but a moment of the tale they will tell. And like all moments of 'deportation', it is an important chapter full of miraculous tales of intervention and grace. But those are tales for another day. Today is the day to remember the end of the story, the arrival of the Serving King, "...and Jacob, the Father of Joseph, the husband of Mary, of whom Jesus was born, who is called the Christ." Love on...
DM

Heritage Matters . . . Or Does It?

"You don't stumble upon your heritage. It's there, just waiting to be explored and shared." —Robbie Robertson

So all the generations from Abraham to David were fourteen generations, and from David to the deportation to Babylon fourteen generations, and from the deportation to Babylon to the Christ fourteen generations.　　　(Matthew 1:17)

This wraps up Matthew's genealogy, an important beginning for any culture understanding the importance of the roots of who we are. It proved helpful to have such a concise way to remember the genealogy of Jesus: 14 generations in 3 sections.

For today's audience, it's fair to ask, "Why does all of this matter?" The point of this orderly record is to suggest that Jesus is the answer to the covenant God made to Abraham. More importantly, perhaps, He is the promised and rightful heir to David's throne. But the list is surprising, filled with less than stellar followers in the Kingdom of God. Why include such a ragtag gathering of people?

I find the answer in Genesis 22:17. At that time, God reaffirmed the covenant and blessed Abraham as he demonstrated incredible obedience in his willingness to sacrifice his son Isaac. God says Abraham's offspring will possess the gate of his enemies. The Jews would have recognized this as a strong statement of their victories to come. History has proven that to be true on many occasions, however, not always. The exile to Babylon depicts defeat rather than victory. This defeat, tragically unnecessary, results from the disobedience of the many people mentioned in the genealogy.

As the genealogy wraps up with the end of the deportation and the birth of Jesus, the promise of victory remains, pointing to Him. We are fortunate to have the whole New Testament. We know that Jesus is the One who fulfills the covenant and the promise of complete victory. He holds the keys to Hades! It was already determined before Abraham began his journey from Ur to Canaan. The people listed in the genealogy absolutely matter, as do you and I, but regardless of their obedience or ours, they themselves do not fulfill or abolish the covenant or the power of the One who so perfectly comes 42 generations after the original promise. We join a long line of those committed to loving like the Serving King...

MR

What's His Name?

"If I'm gonna tell a real story, I'm gonna start with my name." —Kendrick Lamar

"She will bear a son, and you shall call His name Jesus, for He will save His people from their sins." (Matthew 1:21)

When we named our firstborn "Jacob" in the late 1990s, we thought we were doing something unique. No one in our immediate family was named Jacob (there was a great-grandfather in Germany, but we have never met him), and we did not know many people named Jacob, either. As Jacob grew and entered school, started playing baseball, and got involved in other activities, we realized that the name itself was not unique at all. In fact, years later, my wife ran across a list of "most popular names" on the internet, and she discovered that in the year our son was born, Jacob topped the list of most popular names!

The name "Jesus," a derivative of the Old Testament name "Joseph," was also quite popular. The name means, "the LORD saves," and everyone in the time of Jesus—a time when Israel was subject to the pagan government of Rome—longed for the deliverance that God had promised centuries earlier. With so many named "Jesus," or some version of it, what would be different about this boy born in an out-of-the-way backwater village to parents who barely had the resources to deliver themselves, much less a whole nation?

Jesus did live up to His name, however! He separated Himself from all others by walking in harmony with His heavenly Father, by fulfilling the mission He was born for, and by giving His life so that all could come to realize the love of God. Naming a child is a precious and important time. We all pray that the names of our children would be identified with good traits, even if many others share their name. Jesus did more than fulfill the promise of His name, a name originally associated with the deliverance of one nation. Jesus transcends this by being the Deliverer of all nations. The glory of His name, however, was not rooted in a worldly definition. Rather, the name of Jesus is now and forever firmly rooted in doing the will of the Father who sent Him. Through His name and His power, may our identities—regardless of what we are called—be wrapped up in His! Love in the name of the Serving King…
CC

I'm Right Here

"Be strong, be fearless, be beautiful. And believe that anything is possible when you have the right people there to support you." —Misty Copeland

"All this took place to fulfill what the Lord had spoken by the prophet: 'Behold, the virgin shall conceive and bear a son, and they shall call His name Immanuel' (which means, God with us)." (Matthew 1:22-23)

"I'm right here. Don't worry." These are words that good parents speak over and over again to their children. When children fear the dark, are taking their first steps, learning to ride a bike, or are suffering from their first broken heart, good parents are there and quick to remind them: "I'm right here. Don't worry."

God has a long history of speaking such words to His people. "Do not be afraid, I have heard your cries, and I am here." Through the Old Testament, during the most desperate times and situations involving God's people, these words flow. God determined that we needed an even greater reminder than His words of comfort and grace. So, God sent the Living Word: Jesus. He is the living embodiment of comfort, peace, grace, and love. He is God "up close and personal," saying the words: "I am here. Don't worry." Jesus Himself echoed the words, "Do not be afraid," often in His earthly ministry. No wonder this One named "Jesus," which means the "the Lord saves," is also called "Immanuel," which means God with us. When God is around, we have no need to fear or worry, because His very presence brings peace, comfort, and even joy.

Years after these words of anticipation were spoken by the angel, this One who was "God with us" demonstrated once and for all that not even the most frightening thing in human experience—death—could keep God from saying, "Don't worry. I'm here." May we walk in a spirit of peace and joy, leaving fear and despair behind, as we allow the presence of Jesus by His Spirit to give us a comfort and peace that surpasses all comprehension. He's 'right here' as we love like the Serving King…
CC

A Cycle of Obedience

"Obedience brings success; exact obedience brings miracles."—Russell M. Nelson

"When Joseph woke from sleep, he did as the angel of the Lord commanded him: he took his wife, but knew her not until she had given birth to a son. And he called His name Jesus." (Matthew 1:24-25)

Most of us grow up learning not to lie. The reason, as we are told and often end up experiencing, is that one lie leads to another. This is true for sin, as well. One "small" sin (at least small in our eyes) can lead to many bigger sins down the road. One act of disobedience can lead to ongoing rebellion. One act of violence can lead to multiple acts, because violence then becomes the norm. And so on....

The Bible teaches us that human beings have a propensity toward repeated disobedience. We lean in the direction of rebellion, and one act of rebellion against God and God's ways leads to a cycle—a lifestyle—of moving in the opposite direction of God's purposes. The theological phrase associated with this leaning is known as "original sin." We believe that the redemption provided by Jesus through a full surrender to the guidance of the Holy Spirit provides a remedy for original sin. In other words, we believe that the saving and sanctifying work of God through the effort of Jesus and the empowerment of the Holy Spirit leans us back in God's direction. When this happens, though we still have freewill and are able to still say "no" to the purposes of God, we believe that a new cycle occurs: a cycle of obedience. We call this kind of living in a cycle of consistent obedience to God "entire sanctification," and it is modeled for us perfectly in the life of Jesus.

However, we also see glimpses of the powerful works of God that can happen when this cycle of obedience begins, by looking at the response of Jesus' earthly parents! Mary was frightened and overwhelmed when approached by the angel, but she surrendered to the will of God, and by God's grace continued to obey. Joseph was faced with possible humiliation when asked by God through the angel to trust that this child Mary carried was of the Holy Spirit, and he (by God's grace) began a cycle of obedience. The result: Jesus came, and the work of God exploded in new ways in the world. May we allow God's Spirit to begin a new cycle of obedience in us, as we love like the Serving King...
CC

DAY 9

The Why Matters

"After Jesus was born in Bethlehem in Judea, during the time of King Herod, Magi from the east came to Jerusalem and asked, "Where is the One who has been born king of the Jews? We saw His star when it rose and have come to worship Him." When King Herod heard this he was disturbed, and all Jerusalem with him." (Matthew 2:1-3)

We do a lot of things that we say really matter in our lives. However, one thing that we often overlook entirely is 'why we do them'. The 'why' is important. In fact, it can change the entire meaning of what we are doing. One great example is when children are told to say they're sorry. Most children go through the initial stage of crossing their arms and scowling while muttering their dreaded, "Sorry!" Clearly, a mechanical act of obedience.

Now, ask yourself: Are they really sorry? Why are they sorry? The truth typically lays between several answers. Many aren't sorry for anything. Perhaps, they are sorry; sorry they got caught or in trouble. Of course, some really are sorry for their actions and regret them. In the end, the why changes the "Sorry!"

We see the same type of thing in our Scripture. Both the Magi and King Herod were searching for the King of the Jews. However, they had different whys. The Magi had been following the star searching for the King foretold by the prophets. They desired to worship Him. Their why was pure and holy. On the other hand, King Herod was jealous. He didn't want a king messing with his power. He sought out to destroy the baby who was to be King of the Jews.

There was one common goal: Seek and find the newborn king. However, there were also two completely different whys. These whys determine whether the things we do truly matter in the Kingdom of God. Ask yourself, why am I doing the things that I do. Does it draw me closer to the Serving King? Is my obedience genuinely an expression of my loving like the Serving King...
ME

DAY 10

From the Least

"God will meet you where you are in order to take you where He wants you to go."
—Tony Evans

"In Bethlehem in Judea," they replied, "for this is what the prophet has written: 'But you, Bethlehem, in the land of Judah, are by no means least among the rulers of Judah; for out of you will come a ruler who will shepherd my people Israel." (Matthew 2:5-6)

The coming of the Messiah was promised in an unusual way that many overlook. Jesus, the Messiah, the promised Savior and High Priest, came from the tribe of Judah. This broke the mold. Priests came only from the tribe of Levi. Significant change was in the air. This was just one way we see God sending the Christ to break through the old covenant and save through the ultimate sacrifice, the cross of the Serving King, the foundation of the New Covenant.

Jesus, the Son of God, came to us. He met people right where they were. The model He lived showed us not only the love of God, but His love for all of us. Even before we recognize our sin, repent of our sin, embrace the sorrow of our sin, Jesus Christ paid the price for us. His love is comprehensive, encompassing all who are lost in the way of sin.

This gift is offered to all, everyone, a standing invitation awaiting acceptance. No matter what we do, none of us will ever be able to deserve it or pay it back. It is a pure and holy gift offered out of the utterly limitless love of The Divine.

So, what's so important about this particular gift? Jesus, the Son of God, took on human form and came to earth. He lived where we live, walked where we walk. He faced the temptations and trials we do, but He remained holy, blazing a new trail for us. It was only through the suffering, death, and resurrection of the holy and pure Lamb of God that our sins can be forgiven. Believe in Jesus as your Lord and Savior, accept forgiveness. This is the only sacrifice that could truly break the chains of sin, once and for all.

The gift is already offered. Have you accepted the offer of love from the Serving King? Receive His gift and begin a life of loving like the Serving King...
ME

Gifts

"I want to challenge you today to get out of your comfort zone. You have so much incredible potential on the inside. God has put gifts and talents in you that you probably don't know anything about." — Joel Osteen

Then opening their treasures, they offered Him gifts, gold and frankencise and myrrh. (Matthew 2:11)

Christmas always makes me nervous, every eye on me, all waiting for the reaction, my reaction, to the gift released from the paper falling to the floor. The pressure is immense, a tension rising from my gut to my throat, an awareness that for just in the blink of an eye, my reaction to the gift will be genuine, uncontrolled, the real deal. Though it last only for a moment, soon replaced by a heart of gratitude, that initial moment tells the tale: Did he really like the gift? Even at this late stage of the game, I, too, cannot fake that initial moment, my telltale heart showing its true emotion.

The problem, of course, is the gift itself and my desire for certain gifts above others. I try to approach Christmas morning with a full heart, no desire unmet, no wishful thinking as the packages pile in front of me, all waiting to be revealed. But to no avail, at least for me. Lurking in the depths of the heart, or the flesh, are those vestiges of desire, those unwanted longings for just the right this or that. Hiding in the subconscious, only disclosing themselves in the moment of revelation, the sudden awareness of the gift, released from its paper prison. And then it happens, the blink of eye, the revelation of the heart, a momentary delight or frown, soon replaced with the joy of a heart delighted to have been loved by the giver of the gift.

Fortunately for us, there is no gift He needs, no lurking desires of the flesh, no needs clamoring to be met, no unmet longings. No, this is the Serving King, the One who genuinely delights in each and every gift, all of them unneeded, all of them eagerly embraced by Him who delights in our every gift. And yes, we watch Him closely, eager to see His joy as our gift breaks free into His presence. Gold, frankencise, and myrrh, each worthless to the Serving King, each precious to Him, only as gestures of a grateful heart. Fear not, every gift He has stored in you brings joy to the heart of the Serving King. Love on...
DM

Warnings...

"If your watch is slow by just four minutes, that's not much - unless you've been warned that if you're even one minute late ever again you will be fired. Then four minutes make a big difference." —Zig Ziglar

And being warned in a dream not to return to Herod, they departed to their own country by another way...   (Matthew 2:12)

Sometimes warnings are incredibly ostentatious, too big to miss, so obvious even the fool sees them. Some warnings prevent even the densest of fools from traveling farther down the road of misfortune and chaos. Unfortunately, most warnings are far more subtle, mere phantoms of the moment, quickly passing across the conscious mind before flittering into the land of forgetfulness. And, perhaps, the most subtle of all warnings dance in the subconscious, speaking only for a moment before disappearing into the land of dreams.

Dreams, like it or not, are often the screen upon which the communications of God appear, crystal clear in the moment, but soon lost as the conscious mind awakens to engage. The wise men, master dreamers, attentive to the subtleties of dreamland, take seriously the warnings of the subconscious mind, hesitating not to embrace the truths of the sleepy moment. There is no time for debating the flickering warnings of dreamland, the whisperings of the Holy Spirit. This is the moment to engage, to depart, to obey the subtle warnings of dreamland.

Moderns, too devoted to the god of science to ever give heed to 'dreams', quickly dismiss the warnings of dreamland, mandating instead warnings of another kind, warnings easily measured and repeated. Only the ever-present street signs can catch the imagination of moderns who return over and over to the sign, comforted by its stagnant presence.

But God is often a God of the subtle, the illusive, the momentary clarity, gone as quickly as it came. Too often the whisperings of God will appear in the mist, only to fade as the mist disperses into the heat of the day. But wise are those who learn to implement the warnings of the fading moment. Seize it while you can, and never hesitate to engage quickly as you love on...
DM

Does Anybody See What's Going On?

"There aren't just bad people that commit genocide; we are all capable of it. It's our evolutionary history." —James Lovelock

The Herod, when he saw that he had been tricked by the wise men, became furious, and he sent and killed all the male children in Bethlehem and all in the region who were two years old or under... (Matthew 2:13-18)

As I read this passage, my head exploded in frustration and bewilderment. I had so many questions: Does anybody see what is going on? Why is this happening? Why are children being killed and no one is doing anything? Is anybody in charge? Does anybody care? It seems like thousands of children being killed is no big deal, just part of the story. Where is God in the midst of all the chaos?

God could step in and save everything and everyone, but that is not His eternal-providential plan. It doesn't make sense to me, but that is how God set it up, allowed it to unfold. Like Job, we all question, why? We all wonder why God doesn't do more to stop the pain and carnage.

It is difficult for us to see and comprehend the eternal. It is challenging to understand, beyond what we see and experience is an eternal plan to save all mankind. It is difficult to believe that this plan, even this catastrophic event, was defined before God created the world. Proverbs 25:2 tells us that "...it is the glory of God to conceal a matter." It does not matter whether we understand or agree with God's plan: it is His perfect plan. His plan will be executed, no matter the immediate pain or confusion.

This event took place to save one very significant child: Jesus Christ. He is the centerpiece of God's eternal plan of salvation. Beyond what we see and experience, God's plan of salvation is set and being perfectly executed. We may never understand it nor comprehend its depth and efficiency. But no matter what we see or feel, we can count on His plan.

The next time things seem out of control, and it appears no one sees or cares, remember God's plan never fails. No matter how our human mind and emotions may react, God is in control, and His will is accomplished. We don't have to understand it, or even like it, but God will accomplish His plan of salvation in our lives. He does see. He does care. And He will do whatever is necessary to save us for eternity. Love on, even when understanding alludes you...

JL

Too Many Detours

"Perseverance is not a long race; it is many short races one after the other."
—Walter Elliot

**So he got up, took the child and His mother and went to the land of Israel.
But when he heard that Archelaus was reigning in Judea in place of his father
Herod, he was afraid to go there. Having been warned in a dream, he withdrew
to the district of Galilee, and he went and lived in a town called Nazareth.**
(Matt. 2:21-23)

I think Joseph had quite a few days when he felt frustrated. First, his
best-laid plans were ruined by Mary's "early" pregnancy. Despite the
chatter from the community, Joseph remained faithful and followed
what he thought God's will was for his new family. While he could not
know everything that was in store for them, Joseph knew that his Son
was special. He looked forward to what was to come.

Yet, life did not turn out like Joseph thought. He was forced to flee
to Egypt, because the king wanted to kill his new Son. He left all he
had known and went to this new land. Now that Herod was dead, it was
time to return to his home. However, when he returned home, Joseph
discovered the political situation was not safe, so he was forced to move
again, and this time to a place called Nazareth.

It seems there is a lesson in this complicated story. Joseph knew
that God had a special task for his Son. Joseph looked forward to what
this special task was, but life kept interrupting. A royal death threat, a
desperate trip to Egypt, and now an abrupt return and a new detour. This
was not fair. How could God's leading ever come to fruition, if all of
these roadblocks keep getting tossed in their path?

Yet, throughout all of these struggles, God was accomplishing His
great purpose. We should never confuse unexpected difficulty with a
lack of God's presence. We should also never confuse God's silence
for God's inactivity. Underneath all of the twists and turns, something
remarkable was happening to Joseph and his family. Could it be that in
the middle of all of our unexpected detours, something remarkable is
happening as well? As Matthew looks back at this period of Jesus' life,
it all makes sense. Maybe someday our journey will too – if we do not
abandon the journey. Don't give up. Keep loving…
DW

DAY 15

Desert Faith

"Sometimes the most beautiful thing is precisely the one that comes unexpectedly and unearned, hence something given truly as a present."—Anna Freud

In those days John the Baptist came preaching in the desert of Judea and saying, "Repent, for the Kingdom of Heaven is at hand." (Matthew 3:1)

Matthew's account of John the Baptist's ministry begins with "In those days." A 30-year period of time elapsed between the close of Matthew chapter 2 and the opening of Matthew chapter three. Thirty years is a long time to prepare the Messiah for the task ahead.

Matthew has his reasons for arranging the story that way, but he gets right to the task of introducing the Messiah with John's public proclamation in Mathew 3:1. And these events take place in the wilderness of Judea located East of Jerusalem and West of the Dead Sea in the lower Jordan Valley.

'Wilderness' is better translated as 'desert.' Nothing about Jesus' arrival was royal in an earthly sense; He was born in a manger to lowly Mary and lived in Nazareth. Not exactly the kind of arrival anyone would expect for a much-anticipated Messiah. And here is John the Baptist setting the stage for a big announcement—in the desert of all places. Make no mistake, plenty of traffic runs along the edges of the Judean desert; it was a minor highway of sorts, and John takes full advantage of it. He has an audience—in the desert!

When we think of the desert, we think of a desolate place void of anything resembling life. Not so in Matthew's Gospel where the Good News of the Gospel is heard. In Matthew's Gospel, God-activity appears in a place we don't expect. Matthew invites readers to listen as God's Kingdom is proclaimed from an unlikely place—a desert—because God is found in places we don't expect Him to be. It is the way of the Serving King.

Where is your desert? What does your wilderness look like? Where have you forbidden God to go? Our faith is deepened in such places. It is in the desert that God does some of His finest work. Love on, even when you find yourself in the desert…
BH

Non-Prophet Christianity

"The most distressing thing that can happen to a prophet is to be proved wrong. The next most distressing thing is to be proved right." —Aldous Huxley

But when he saw many of the Pharisees and Sadducees coming to his baptism, he said to them, "You brood of vipers! Who warned you to flee the coming wrath?"
(Matthew 3:7)

John the Baptist was a prophet at a time in Israel's history when there were none. Silence ruled the land for a very long time. And then there was John the Baptist ready to invade the silence, to usher in the age of the Serving King.

He took an unusual stand against the religious leaders by calling them a "brood of vipers." The obtainment of personal popularity and political power were not of concern to John. He was willing to stand alone in denouncing all that was wrong with the religious establishment. He was willing to speak while others remained silent. The prophet Isaiah described John as "the voice of one crying in the wilderness to prepare the way of the Lord" (Isaiah 40:33). John was a true prophet in the tradition of Moses, Elijah, and Isaiah delivering a message strange to peoples' ears. Unwilling to shy away from the truth, John was truly a great man who, according to Jesus, was the greatest of all prophets (Matt. 11:11).

John the Baptist may have served his purpose 2,000 years ago, but is there a place for modern-day prophets? John the Baptist types are hard to come by, and the church, it seems, has become a non-prophetic organization. Mandatory diets and dress codes are not necessary to minister like John the Baptist; rather, a willingness to stand alone and speak the truth.

Are you an against-the-grain type of person like John? Willing to take an unpopular stand and go it alone if necessary? What is the truth you need to speak, as you dare to love like the Serving King…
BH

Repentance vs. Remorse

"Regret is not a proactive feeling. It is situated in disappointment, sorrow, even remorse. It merely wishes things were different without an act to cause a difference. However, repentance is different. Repentance is an admission of, hatred of, and turning away from sin before God." —Monica Johnson

"Bear fruit in keeping with repentance." (Matthew 3:8)

John the Baptist delivered a message of repentance, the necessity of a radical and profound change of heart, followed by water baptism. But what is repentance, and does it impact how we respond to an angry God threatening judgment? Is it a reminder to shape up?

John's message of repentance was accompanied by an invitation to experience the grace of forgiveness. Curiosity seekers were likely among those in the crowd, but many came seeking genuine transformation. Repentance need not be something chosen out of fear; rather, a willful turning for the better; a hopeful pursuit.

Repentance, however, should not be confused with temporary feelings of remorse. It is more than acknowledging one's sinful state and momentarily confessing it. Repentance involves a permanent change of mind flowing into the condition of the heart. And transformed hearts cannot help but insist on obedience.

John speaks to this idea in Matthew 3:8, "produce fruit in keeping with repentance." He understood a transformed heart and mind would usher in a lasting change supported by action-- a far cry from just being sorry. A fervent commitment to change is more consistent with the idea of repentance. Replacing old habits, outdated ways and attitudes over the course of time make it possible to produce the fruit to which John points. When we do our part in turning to God, we are never the same as God produces lasting change in us.

How do you think about repentance? Of what do you need to repent? How is repentance an opportunity to become a better you, as you keep loving on…

BH

Wilderness Hope

"Love recognizes no barriers. It jumps hurdles, leaps fences, penetrates walls to arrive at its destination full of hope". —Maya Angelou

"I baptize you with water for repentance, but He who is coming after me is mightier than I, whose sandals I am not worthy to carry. He will baptize you with the Holy Spirit and fire. (Matthew 3:11)

As a wilderness man, John's survival was tied to a steady diet of locusts and wild honey. He wore a garment made of camel's hair with a leather belt around his waist. It was a peculiar way of life leading some to believe that John found himself among an austere sect of people in a place called Qumran. Out of devotion to God and concern for Israel, the Qumran community retreated to the wilderness. They believed things had gotten so bad that a radical change was needed. An erosion of trust in the religious system of their day prompted the formation of a tight-knit community that would hope in a Messiah.

John's likely association with Qumran took a unique turn when he revealed the Messiah's identity. John pointed people to Jesus, not himself. Unlike other messianic movements that failed to deliver, John presented hearers with the fleshly embodiment of his message. To his followers, John says, "I baptize you with water for repentance, but He who is coming after me is mightier than I, whose sandals I am not worthy to carry. He will baptize you with the Holy Spirit and fire" (Matt. 3:11). Words that resonated deeply when Jesus stood among them.

This is what I love about John! He points hearers of his message to the One in whom all hope is found. Deflecting attention away from himself, John delivers Jesus to a broken and frustrated people longing for change. And this is John's message to us: hope is a Person and His name is Jesus.

Where is hope needed in your life today? How are you realizing this hope when everything seems hopeless? Hope will empower you as you love on…

BH

When the Godly Resist God

"Faith that it's not always in your hands or things don't always go the way you planned, but you have to have faith that there is a plan for you."
—Martina McBride

Jesus came...to John, to be baptized by him. John would have prevented Him, saying, "I need to be baptized by You, and do You come to me?" But Jesus answered him, "Let it be so now, for thus it is fitting for us to fulfill all righteousness." And when Jesus was baptized...and behold, a voice from heaven said, "This is My beloved Son, with whom I am well pleased."

(Matthew 3:13-17)

One cannot be sure if it was the tone in His voice, the look in His eye, or the logic of His words, but what we do know for certain was that Jesus quickly overcame the resistance He encountered. We can also be sure that Jesus had not arrived at the muddy Jordan River by happenstance, nor was it a last moment decision for Him to be baptized. He had purposefully made the long, arduous journey from Galilee to the Jordan River for the specific purpose of being baptized by John. John, however, was not in tune with Jesus' plan. The request created an immediate crisis of conscience. Based on John's future question to Jesus (Matthew 11:3), it is uncertain whether John had already concluded that Jesus was the Messiah, but he did recognize Him as someone more important than himself. As such, his logic dictated to him that he was not worthy to perform this baptism, but, instead, he should be receiving baptism from Jesus.

How often does our logic cause us to resist the plan of God for our lives? We take our limited knowledge of the circumstances and our frequently clouded perspective and conclude that the plan of God is misguided, and so we resist. We offer to God what we perceive to be a better plan. If we listen closely in those moments, we will hear the words of Jesus to John echo in our ear, "let this be so now" – now before we understand the reason it is the best for us. The word 'now' also communicates urgency. Most of the time, there is a time frame in which we must enact God's plan.

By John's obedience, Jesus and John fulfilled all righteousness. It was a fulfillment of the Father's will that Jesus be baptized and that John would be the baptizer. And through this righteous obedience, the stage was set for the proclamation, "This is My beloved Son, with whom I am well pleased." Dare to love like the Serving King...
DS

The Beginning of Greatness

"A fast is not a hunger strike. Fasting submits to God's commands. A hunger strike makes God submit to our demands." —Edwin Louis Cole

Then Jesus was led by the Spirit into the wilderness to be tempted by the devil. After fasting forty days and forty nights, He was hungry. (Matthew 4:1-2)

Following His baptism, Jesus experienced an incredible spiritual mountaintop that many of us only dream. Yet, that mountaintop would not last. The very Spirit that split the heavens and alighted upon Jesus would now lead Him into the desert for a fast lasting 40 days, followed by an incredibly difficult period of temptation. The Holy Spirit knew Jesus would be tempted, however, that does not mean God deserted Him, nor is the Spirit the One who tempted Him. James 1:13 reminds us that God does not tempt men as even Satan can do nothing the Father does not allow.

But what happened during the 40 days of Temptation? While the Bible does not tell us anything about the time before the temptations, what we know from tradition is that Jesus would have been spending time with the Father being strengthened in His inner man, becoming acutely aware of God's purposes. That was, after all, the reason to fast. Clearly, the Father met Jesus during the 40 days, because He wasn't hungry until it was all over. Therefore, I think it's fair to say the 40 days were a time of building up and preparation. Do not be confused thinking this was a time where Jesus became weaker and weaker as the days and nights went by. That is never the purpose of a fast, and we have no reason to believe that would have happened or been the purpose when the Holy Spirit led Jesus to this moment.

We should understand that as Jesus comes to the end of His fast, He is spiritually stronger than ever! He is closer to the Father and acutely attuned to what the Father desires. This may be the beginning of Jesus abiding so closely with the Father that He would later say He only does what He sees the Father doing or say what the Father is saying. The fast gave Him the spiritual fortitude to successfully walk through the temptations. Perhaps, more importantly, it prepared Him for the walk of love awaiting Him in the days to come. Have you prepared yourself as you step into a life of loving like the Serving King…
MR

Tempting the Bread of Life

"Temptation is the devil looking through the keyhole. Yielding is opening the door and inviting him in." —Billy Sunday

The tempter came to Him and said, "If you are the Son of God, tell these stones to become bread." Jesus answered, "It is written: 'Man shall not live on bread alone, but on every word that comes from the mouth of God.'" (Matthew 4:3-4)

It makes sense from a human standpoint that Satan would tempt Jesus with bread, because at this point, He is admittedly physically hungry. However, do not forget that while His body was hungry, He was spiritually filled after 40 days of incredible intimacy with the Father. Jesus spoke from experience when He later said that those who hunger and thirst for righteousness would be satisfied (Matthew 5:6). He had the spiritual mettle to not cave to the temptation of bread.

Even more than all of that, Jesus proves in this first temptation that He knew exactly who He was. He was confident in His identity as the Son of Man and the Bread of Life! In John 6:33-51, Jesus told His followers four times that He is the Bread of Life. Consider that Satan offered bread to the One who is the Bread of Life! That was not His most brilliant move! Jesus is the bread! How could He accept the temporary satisfaction Satan had to offer? Jesus knew it was a ploy and a lie. That's why His response was so perfect. Jesus was living off the words from the Father for 40 days. He was filled!

We must consider this carefully, because the concept applies to us as followers of Jesus. Satan will tempt us with bread if we are hungry. While we are not the Bread of Life, we know the One who is and He lives in us! If we know Jesus as Savior, we must also know who we are in Him. As children of the Bread of Life, we can turn down the temptations that only provide temporary satisfaction and instead feast on the One who satisfies completely and forever. Knowing our identity in Christ is critical to our ability to say with confidence to the tempter that we do not live by bread alone, but by the very words of God Himself. Love drives us to extreme behavior, when we love like the Serving King…
MR

Staying on the Right Path

"We usually know what we can do, but temptation shows us who we are."
—Thomas a Kempis

Then the devil took Him to the holy city and had Him stand on the highest point of the temple. "If You are the Son of God," he said, "throw Yourself down. For it is written: "He will command His angels concerning You, and they will lift You up in their hands, so that You will not strike Your foot against a stone." Jesus answered him, "It is also written: 'Do not put the Lord your God to the test.'"

(Matthew 4:5-7)

Once again, Satan is challenging Jesus' identity as the Son of God. This time, it seems Satan wants Jesus to test the prophecy of divine protection as stated in Psalm 91:11-12. Jesus knew this was not the way prophecy would be played out, for He was already aware of what lay ahead three years later when He would go to the cross.

But, there is more to this temptation than simply testing Jesus' identity and prophecy concerning Him. Consider what would have happened, if Jesus did throw Himself down from the highest point of the temple and somehow gently land on His feet. Perhaps, this was more in line with what the people expected, as they wanted the Messiah to be a strong military leader. Such a grand beginning to His ministry would have certainly gained attention and portrayed some sort of power. Yet, we know from history that was not the way of Jesus. He did lead in strength and power, but it was not as the world would define it. He led by being a servant and demonstrating love, healing the sick, raising the dead, and submitting to authorities.

Consider also that Jesus' ministry was never meant to begin with a sensational entrance. Perhaps, Satan was really tempting Jesus to skip the next three years and everything they set into motion such as Satan's destruction and public humiliation as described in Philippians 2:15. If he could get Jesus to forget the way to the cross, he would have a future instead.

This type of temptation is not exclusive to Jesus. We are tempted to forsake the path God puts before us, so Satan will have more time and influence on the earth. However, every time we choose to walk as the Father leads instead of as Satan tempts, we are putting him closer to his last days. If you feel like Satan pushes harder against you when you are abiding in Christ, you are probably correct. However, even though Satan may come to steal, kill, and destroy, Jesus came that we may have abundant life as we love on...

MR

The Lie of the World

"Knowledge of God's Word is a bulwark against deception, temptation, accusation, even persecution." —Edwin Louis Cole

Again, the devil took Him to a very high mountain and showed Him all the kingdoms of the world and their splendor. "All this I will give You," he said, "if You will bow down and worship me." Jesus said to him, "Away from Me, Satan! For it is written: 'Worship the Lord your God and serve Him only. Then the devil left Him, and angels came and attended Him. (Matthew 4:8-11)

If this wasn't such a serious temptation, it would be laughable. Satan, once again, tempts Jesus with something He already has! In Psalm 2:8, the Father tells Jesus all He has to do is ask and the nations, even to the ends of earth, are His inheritance! Of course, the kicker in Satan's temptation is that Jesus would have to worship him. Jesus knew that one day every knee would bow and every tongue confess that He is Lord. He had no need to worship Satan, and He knew Satan could not really give Him the world. Once again, Jesus knew the Father's plan was perfect.

Even though I am tempted to laugh at how dumb Satan was in this final temptation, I am more apt to cry when I consider how easy we fall prey to the same temptation. Most of us have in some way, bowed down to Satan for the prize of the world and its offerings. Many of us raising children want to make sure they have everything at their fingertips all the time! We literally want to give them the world and many take painstaking steps to do so.

We must remember that to gain the world and everything in it, we are bowing down to Satan and forsaking the inheritance that is already ours as believers in Jesus the Messiah. What is the remedy? Respond as Jesus responded. Start every day, really every moment, in a heart posture of worship and adoration to the Lord your God and serve Him only. When you are making a decision to buy something, go somewhere, or give something to someone else, test that decision by asking if or how God is honored in your decision. If there is no honor for God, it is likely a veiled act of devotion to the tempter.

Know who you are in Christ. He is the Bread of Life, feast on Him. He is the Messiah, abide in Him. His ways are not of this world, but they are everlasting. Worship and serve Him only as you love on…
MR

DAY 24

Be Comforted!

"I've learned in my life that it's important to be able to step outside your comfort zone and be challenged with something you're not familiar or accustomed to."
—*J. R. Martinez*

Now when He heard that John had been arrested, He withdrew into Galilee. And leaving Nazareth He went and lived in Capernaum by the sea, in the territory of Zebulun and Naphtali, so that what was spoken by the prophet Isaiah might be fulfilled: "The land of Zebulun and the land of Naphtali, the way of the sea, beyond the Jordan, Galilee of the Gentiles— the people dwelling in darkness have seen a great light, and for those dwelling in the region and shadow of death, on them a light has dawned." (Matthew 4:12-16)

After Jesus was tempted in the wilderness, "Angels came and were ministering to Him." He then chose to move from His hometown of Nazareth, approximately 30 miles to the seaside city of Capernaum. He did this after hearing of John's arrest; yet, Scripture does not say why exactly He moved. An angel did not appear telling Him to move. His disciples did not tell Him to go, as He had not chosen any disciples at this time. Was He in fear for His life? Like John, did He feel He could be arrested? Scripture does not say. He simply picked Himself up and moved. What we do know is that He fulfilled Old Testament Scripture, Isaiah 9:1-2, when He said in Matthew 4:15-16, "The land of Zebulun and the land of Naphtali, the way of the sea, beyond the Jordan, Galilee of the Gentiles— the people dwelling in darkness have seen a great light, and for those dwelling in the region and shadow of death, on them a light has dawned."

When have you been tempted? How has the devil schemed to steal your attention from the Lord Jesus? What has the devil promised? Have you found yourself in a place of darkness or in the "shadow of death?" Well, there is Good News. Jesus moved to the City of Capernaum which literally means "City of Consolation," or as Hitchcock's Bible Names Dictionary describes, "the city of comfort." Jesus sent us His Spirit, the Holy Spirit, our Comforter. We don't need to go someplace in search of hope, healing, inspiration, or comfort. We have the Holy Spirit right where we are. So, has the devil promised you fortune, friends, or fame but delivered nothing? Then be comforted by the Great Light who delivers us the promise of eternal life as we love like the Serving King...
JP

State Of Mind

"The Kingdom of Heaven is not a place, but a state of mind."
— *John Burroughs*

From that time Jesus began to preach, saying, "Repent for the Kingdom of Heaven is at hand." (Matthew 4:17)

Tomorrow, and all that it brings with it, is a long way off. But not nearly so far off as you might imagine. Such is the reality of the arrival of the Kingdom of Heaven. As the saying goes, "It is here, but not yet." Still, the not yet is closer than we have imagined. And with its arrival comes the necessity of change, not just in the 'state of mind', but in the mundane of life as well.

For those who sense its presence, this Kingdom of Heaven, life can never be the same. It is the realization, firmly perceived and sensed in the mind, of the impending arrival, initiating the introduction of the Kingdom. It unfolds in the life of those who have taken the first step, accepting the necessity of repentance, a profound change of mind unleashing staggering changes in the behavior of those who have sensed the presence of the Kingdom of Heaven. It is they who bring about change, who transform their behavior, step-by-step, renewal crashing down upon those who have welcomed the arrival of the Kingdom.

And this 'state of mind', the arrival of the Kingdom of Heaven, is never content to linger in the minds of those who have welcomed the Kingdom of Heaven. To the contrary, it mandates the creation of a place, small as it may be, where the principles of the Kingdom of Heaven unleash themselves, radically transforming this 'place', the space surrounding those who have embraced this Kingdom.

Such is the nature of the Kingdom of Heaven, with its "here, but not yet." Its arrival begins in the mind and slowly or, perhaps, quickly, for some, transforming the mundane realities of life in the world as we know it. Repentance has arrived. A change of mind has begun. Its work is just beginning. But begin it has. The 'place', once the domain of the mind, is now appearing around those who have embraced the arrival of the Kingdom of Heaven. Love on...
DM

Immediately

"Many men go fishing all of their lives without knowing that it is not fish they are after." —Henry David Thoreau

And He said to them, "Follow Me and I will make you fishers of men." Immediately they left their nets and followed Him. (Matthew 4:18-22)

Few are those whose lives of triviality are interrupted by the invitation to significance. Fewer still, those who recognize the interruption and immediately seize the invitation. Simon and Andrew were two such men. The arrival of Jesus provides a sudden insight into life, an opportunity to recognize life is never really about the fish at all; instead, a glorious opportunity to recognize life for what it is, a practice ground for the life that really matters, the life that is yet to come. And, once recognized, fishing for fish, the mundane of life, simply no longer captivates, no longer provides meaning to life. So the first of many make the 'immediately' decision to change course, to pursue the significant, to seize the precious moment that has arrived.

Thoreau rightly understood the necessity of fishing, not the recreational moment of leisure, rather, the relentless pursuit of the mundane, life's demand to eat or die. He rightly understood all people die, regardless of how many fish they catch. Death is the ultimate destination for all of us. Thus, he lamented the fate of most people, perhaps, even himself, a life wasted on the mundane.

But there are those few who finally discover fish are never the real pursuit, instead, only a distraction from that which really matters in life, a necessity preventing most people from ever pursuing significance. And yet, here you are, pursuing the Serving King, perhaps, even hearing His call to finally 'fish' for ultimate significance.

Life offers no greater gift than the moment of understanding, hearing the Serving King's invitation to put down your rod and reel and join Him in the quest for significance. Shall you too 'immediately' trek on after the Serving King. Love on…
DM

Healing

"Healing is a matter of time, but it is sometimes also a matter of opportunity."
— *Hippocrates*

...and healing every disease and every affliction among the people. So, His fame spread throughout all Syria, and they brought Him all the sick, those afflicted with various diseases and pains, those oppressed by demons, those having seizures, and paralytics, and He healed them. (Matthew 4:22-24)

Like most pastors, I ache for those who are ill, battling the frailties of life. It is a game I know we will all lose, sooner or later. I, too, have watched as good friends, people who profoundly loved God with great faith, withered away under the catastrophic effects of sickness. And like so many, agonized as God remained silent until the final moment. Death claiming its prize, like it always does.

Conversely, I have also watched as others, some who loved God passionately, and some who barely acknowledged the reality of God, experienced amazing stays of execution, at least for the moment. And yes, every healing is just for the moment. Death always claims its prize in the end, but that, too, only for the moment.

Thus, the question of 'why' always rises to the surface. Why does God move so miraculously in the lives of some, but not so in others? It is the haunting question for every person of faith. Some, trying to protect the image of God, place the blame squarely on us...either a lack of faith, or knowledge, or unconfessed sin, etc. But in the end, it is always about us, our failure. Others, never experiencing the miraculous movement of God, attribute healing to 'good genes' or some other form of intervention.

But what if there is more to the story? What if God is at work in all circumstances, both the healing and the non-healing? What if God is really about "...His fame spread throughout all Syria"? Perhaps, those who die well, and those who are healed well, equally contribute to "His fame spread." As Hippocrates suggest, "Healing is a matter of time..." And, for some, that time is in the moment of death. Love on till that final moment arrives...

DM

They Came To Him

"Socrates' fame spread all over Greece, and the most respected and educated men from all around came to him, in order to enjoy his friendly company and instruction." — Moses Mendelssohn

Seeing the crowds, He went up on the mountain, and when He sat down, His disciples came to Him. (Matthew 5:1-2)

People of great wisdom are rarely found, but when they are, wise is the person smart enough to stay on their heels, following them whenever possible. Jesus was clearly one of those people. More importantly, His disciples were wise enough to stay close while the opportunity presented itself. For wise people are often on the move, planting seeds of wisdom across the land as they move.

So comes the challenge to stay on His heels, to sit when He sits, walk when He walks. But life is full of distractions, all clamoring for your attention as the Serving King strolls along the way. And unlike those early disciples, you have not had the luxury of 'leaving everything' behind for this chase after the Serving King. No, yours is a journey filled with interruptions, each important, each demanding your attention.

Fortunately, He understands. Then comes that moment as He reclines on the mountainside, waiting for your return, patience one of His virtues. Still, He will not wait forever; there are too many others waiting to sit at His feet, to hear His words of wisdom. You, too, will have to make a decision to 'come to Him', if even for the moment, to sit at His feet and listen carefully as the Master speaks.

Understand, while you sit quietly at His feet, the noise of life will clamor endlessly in your ear, demanding you return from the mountainside, insisting you deal with the relentless mundane of life. But know this, the wisdom He provides is for the mundane, the life you must live, the world as you experience. He is equipping you for the noise of life, the mundane that demands so much of your time and energy. Join the others at His feet, ready for this daily moment. Life will wait for you, delighted you have returned with wisdom from the Serving King as you love on…

DM

Poverty and Humility, One and the Same?

"He must increase, but I must decrease." —John the Baptist

"Blessed are the poor in spirit, for theirs is the Kingdom of Heaven."

(Matthew 5:3)

"Blessed are the poor in spirit, for theirs is the Kingdom of Heaven." I am not sure if you are like me, but when first reading that passage, I wonder if this does not seem to be something more akin to being cursed than blessed! How can one be 'poor' and 'blessed' at the same time? Seemingly, a real paradox. James 1:5 says, "If any of you lacks wisdom, let him ask God, who gives generously to all without reproach, and it will be given him."

The word 'poor' is actually better translated 'humble', as in destitute in and of themselves. And we understand humility of heart is key to overcoming the despondency of life. In the Book of Palms, 51:17, we find these words, 'The sacrifices of God are a broken spirit; a broken and contrite heart, O God, You will not despise."

Gills Exposition of the Entire Bible suggests of David's Psalm; "The sacrifices of God are a broken spirit that is humbled under a sense of sin; has true repentance for it; is smitten, wounded, and broken with it, by the Word of God in the hand of the Spirit; grieving for sin as committed against a God of love; broken and melted down under a sense of it, in a view of pardoning grace; and mourning for it, while beholding a pierced and wounded Savior: the sacrifices of such a broken heart and contrite spirit are the sacrifices God desires, approves, accepts of, and delights in; a broken and a contrite heart, O God, thou wilt not despise; but regard, and receive with pleasure."

This is what Scripture refers to when it declares, "Blessed are the poor in spirit, for theirs is the Kingdom of Heaven." When you and I begin to realize our life is more about 'Him' and less about 'ourselves or them', the closer (more broken) to the Lord we become. It is they who are 'poor in spirit' who best learn to trek after Him as they love on...
TM

DAY 30

The Conditioner Of The Heart

"Man's inhumanity to man makes countless thousands mourn." — Robert Burns

"Blessed are those who mourn for they shall be comforted." (Matthew 5:4)

Feelings have become the foundation for so much of life in the modern era. Gone are the days when 'feelings' played a distant second fiddle to 'what ought to be done'. Instead, feelings have become a dominant motivator behind the actions of the many. The broad range of feelings now driving the behavior of the many, rendering them slaves to the emotions of the moment.

More tragic, perhaps, is the rush to remove any unwanted feeling, especially the dreaded moment of mourning. The epidemic of over-the-counter narcotics is the by-product of a people who refuse to micromanage their feelings, to move beyond living according to how one feels. Thus, the fruit of mourning is surrendered, lost to a generation refusing to suffer. Sedated, this generation muddles along, weighed down by an inability to mourn, never learning the lessons that only mourning can bring.

Mourning has long been the 'conditioner of the heart', the means by which the heart is broken, softened, and prepared for lessons that can only be learned through the passage of mourning. It is on the other side of mourning that comfort is found, a comfort that heals and prepares the heart for what yet lies ahead in life. It is the once broken and wounded heart, now healed, that learns to love and to embrace the wounded ones still suffering through the days of mourning.

In a land of so much inhumanity, opportunities for mourning are never in short supply. Mourners abound, each wounded in their own unique way, each longing for healing and redemption. And arrive the people of God, once mourners themselves, now healed, offering hope to those still mourning. Mourning is never the last chapter of the tale; rather, it's the precursor to healing and redemption. Love on in the ways of the Serving King. Your healing is just ahead as you love on…
DM

Meek

"If there is anybody in this land who thoroughly believes that the meek shall inherit the earth they have not often let their presence be known." —W. E. B. Du Bois

"Blessed are the meek, for they will inherit the earth."   (Matthew 5:5)

Meekness is sometimes described as strength under control. One appropriate metaphor for meekness is that of a well-trained horse, a creature of immense power, guided by the gentle reins in the hands of its rider. This is a picture of how we as Christians ought to be strong and courageous, yet submissive to the will and movement of God in our lives. In the Sermon on the Mount, Jesus delivered some of His most poignant teachings about how His followers were to live, but the sermon was not limited to these few chapters in the Gospel of Matthew—Jesus' entire life was an embodiment of the message delivered there on the mountain.

How did Jesus demonstrate meekness throughout His life? When His time came to be baptized, Jesus humbled Himself under the authority of John the Baptist (Matt. 3:13–15). When He had the power of God to heal, He did so not for His own glory but for the well-being of people who needed hope (Matt. 8:1–4). When His friends feared for their lives on the Sea of Galilee, He spoke to calm the storm (Matt. 8:23–27). When He was asked to leave a place, He left in peace with dignity (Matt. 8:34–9:1, 10:12–14). When He was challenged on the authority of God He had been given, He countered with a firm rebuttal (Matt. 12:22–32). When He saw money changers taking advantage of devoted Jews, He drove them out of the Temple (Matt. 21:12–13). When His closest friends betrayed Him, He responded with compassion and grace (Matt. 26:31–46). And in the ultimate demonstration of meekness, when His life was threatened, He willfully submitted Himself to death on a cross (Matt. 27:39–54).

Through Jesus' life, we see a picture of meekness that, like the metaphor of the horse, is strength under control. Yet, we also see that, for Jesus, this power was oriented toward the well-being of His neighbors. Jesus constantly worked to improve the lives of the people around Him, restoring their health, their dignity, and their hope. The meekness we are called to is a power that pours itself out—not for our own benefit, but for the benefit of the disenfranchised in our communities. By giving ourselves up in this way, we inherit the earth. Meekness is the way of those who dare to love on...

RG

You Are What You Eat

"Wanting something is not enough. You must hunger for it. Your motivation must be absolutely compelling in order to overcome the obstacles that will invariably come your way." —Les Brown

"Blessed are those who hunger and thirst for righteousness, for they shall be satisfied." (Matthew 5:6)

One of the most common New Year's Resolutions people make is the resolution to lose weight. This normally manifests itself with a renewed commitment to eating healthy and exercising. Sadly, as most of us know, these resolutions often go unrealized, as after some time, the commitment is abandoned and the old habits are resumed.

At the end of the day, the truth is many of us don't really want the things we try to convince ourselves we desire. The list of things I can want is limitless, but the manifestation of how badly I want them is always in the proverbial 'proof in the pudding'. Do I actually do it? Do I actually follow through? Do I really want it bad enough to bring it about? And, if not, what is it my actions prove I really do want versus what I wish I wanted? Do I really want to eat healthy, or do I really want the bowl of ice cream?

If you're like me, eating healthy isn't something that comes easy. I have to fight my natural impulses to consume the sweetest or most fattening things I can find. But I've heard that there are some strange people out there who actually enjoy eating health food.

It could be said, blessed are those who hunger and thirst for healthy food and drink, for they shall be healthy. And those people really are lucky, for good health will be more easily attained by them due to their natural enjoyment of health food.

Hunger and thirst are primal urges, and we go to the utmost of extremes to fill those impulses. Like health food, righteousness is an acquired taste for most of us, a pursuit of discipline and self-control, but, occasionally, there are those whose natural impulse and desire is to acquire this noble trait. Therefore, blessed are those who really do hunger and thirst for righteousness, for righteousness will be more easily attained by those who are born to desire it. Perhaps, loving like the Serving King creates that impulse to hunger after righteousness…
WH

Who Goes First

"Sweet mercy is nobility's true badge." —William Shakespeare

"Blessed are the merciful, for they shall receive mercy." (Matthew 5:7)

Stories of mercy inspire the soul, reminding us of 'nobility's sweetest badge'. And we love the tales of mercy, offering us hope, hope that someday we, too, will be the recipient of mercy, unmerited forgiveness in our moment of judgment. So, we cherish the yarns of mercy, glorious reminders of the power of grace in a land filled with humanity's inhumanity to one another.

But mercy never comes easy for those paying the bill for mercy. Such was the fate of the Serving King who paid the bill for each of us, the debt we deserved, crushing Him in that fateful moment upon the cross. It is here, at the foot of the cross, that we discover the cost of mercy. It is only at the cross that we are reminded that mercy always has a price. Someone must always pay the bill. And yes, it is often expensive, more expensive than we have imagined.

And so, the answer to the question, "Who goes first?" He did, the Serving King, setting the model for all those who would chase after Him. And you, too, will have opportunity to pay the bill for another, to model the power of grace, to mimic the ways of the Serving King.

So comes His proclamation, His summons for all who would chase after Him, "Blessed are those who finally decide to pay the bill for someone else." It is in that moment that you will also have opportunity to extend mercy to another, to pay their bill, simply because Jesus first paid yours. Thus, the contagious nature of mercy begins to flow, unleashing the power of grace as the people of God extend mercy to others equally undeserving in that moment of judgment. He has gone first. Who will be next in line, as you love on in the ways of the Serving King...
DM

When

"A good head and a good heart are always a formidable combination."
—*Nelson Mandela*

"Blessed are the pure in heart, for they shall see God." (Matthew 5:8)

I suspect most of us hear these words in the future tense, a very distant future, one lurking beyond the realms of the here and now. But what if the Serving King was offering an avenue into the present moment, the right here, right now? What if Jesus offers us a foundation for seeing and hearing God more profoundly than we have ever imagined?

Nothing is more dangerous to the status quo than the presence of those who have 'heard' and 'seen' God. They are the most dangerous of all beings to the status quo. It is they who march boldly and confidently, daring to change their world, to take chances no one else is ready to take. Why? Simply because they have 'seen' God. It is they who are confident in the ways of the Serving King. It is they who hear the specifics of how God would have them to act in the particulars of the present moment. Hearing Him, seeing Him, they now march boldly into His way of being and doing.

As Mandela so rightly understood, those who have a 'good head and a good heart' are always the most formidable to the status quo. Empowered by having 'seen' and 'heard' God, they are now ready to change the world, to usher in the Kingdom of God.

The pathway to 'hearing and seeing' God is the way of the pure heart, a heart consumed with pursuing His way of being. And those who dare to look, to see God, to hear God, unleash a power upon their community like no other. They usher in the Kingdom of God, right now, right here. And once you have truly heard Him, seen Him, there can be no turning back. Walk boldly into the future awaiting those chasing after the Serving King…

DM

Labels

"What really matters is how God sees me. He isn't concerned with labels; he is concerned about the state of man's soul." —Billy Graham

"Blessed are the peacemakers, for they shall be called sons of God."

(Matthew 5:9)

Labels are powerful, and never more so than in the modern era. The mantra of previous generations, "Sticks and stones may break my bones, but words can never hurt me," has quietly disappeared, surrendered to a culture offended at every utterance. But with this empowering of mere 'words' has come a new power, the power of labels. And none more powerful than "Sons of God." Imagine carrying the label, "Sons of God." And not because you chose the label; rather, others chose it for you, an apt descriptor of your presence in the community.

So, the question, "Do labels create actions, or do actions create labels?" Here, Jesus reminds us of the power of actions in creating labels. And no action more powerful than that of 'peacemaker', the ability to bring peace in the land of chaos and inhumanity. It is the peacemakers who mimic His presence, creating a new way of being.

But for all our talk of peace, even our lusting after peace, it rarely seems to appear, even in the mundane of everyday life. Perhaps, like mercy, peace is simply too expensive for the masses. It requires a surrendering of rights, authentic rights, rights we are entitled to. Therein lies the problem; an unwillingness to surrender personal rights and privileges for the sake of peace.

Only those empowered by the abiding presence of God seem to have the ability to surrender personal rights and privileges, all for the sake of peace. This surrendering is the telltale sign of those chasing after the Serving King. It is their moniker, their way of being and doing, a way so distinctive only the label 'Sons of God' does it justice. Thus, the challenge of Jesus to make peace and earn the label 'Sons of God', as you love on in the way the Serving King…

DM

DAY 36

Holy Thorns

"I beg you be persuaded that no one would be more zealous than myself to establish effectual barriers against the horrors of spiritual tyranny, and every species of religious persecution." —George Washington

"Blessed are those who are persecuted for righteousness' sake, for theirs is the Kingdom of Heaven." (Matthew 5:10)

Persecution is the litmus test of a holy life. It is a signal to the disciple of Christ that they have forsaken the systems around them that have sought to funnel them to the path of least resistance - the road of compromise, comfort, and spiritual immobility. The clarion call of the Christian to a pattern of self-denial and full devotion to the ways of God is a 'thorn in the side' of a hedonistic society that desires for everything and everyone to "go with the flow." When doing what feels best in the moment is challenged by a lifestyle of holiness, others are quick to tear down anyone that, even in love, presents a counter to their comfort. We're not exempt from this, even in our own churches.

Notice, Christ does not celebrate persecution for persecution's sake. God does not revel in our hardships; in fact, if we believe the words of Romans 8:28, God is working for our good in all things. Persecution on its own is no blessing. We're not to seek out persecution just for the sake of being a social irritant. But persecution endured for the sake of doing right? That is a blessing, indeed. We follow in the footsteps of the Holy One who endured ultimate persecution on account of His righteousness and love.

Have you been under duress for the sake of Christ? Have you ever had your reputation challenged, your work discredited, and your intentions misinterpreted, because the outward expression of your firm convictions was unpopular to a world captive to its own ever-changing standards? As the epistle of James so properly puts it, count it all joy! Why? Resistance to the Gospel is verification that you're traveling the narrow road that leads to salvation. Others are being faced with the truth your life so unashamedly displays. Blessed are the persecuted who walk in righteousness. You're not only heirs of the Kingdom, but its earthly ambassadors as you seek to love like the Serving King…
DR

Risky Business

"There is a time for risky love. There is a time for extravagant gestures. There is a time to pour out your affections on one you love. And when the time comes - seize it, don't miss it." —Max Lucado

Blessed are you when others revile you and persecute you and utter all kinds of evil against you falsely on my account. Rejoice and be glad, for your reward is great in heaven, for so they persecuted the prophets who were before you.

(Matthew 5:11-12)

To this day, I still have awful memories of my ninth grade English class; I'm sure others can relate. I have a specific memory of learning how to write essays for the first time. We had come to the part where we were learning what a thesis statement is and how it is the key statement that holds everything else together. In Matthew's Gospel, the Beatitudes would be considered the "thesis statement" of Jesus. Everything else that Jesus says and does throughout the book is to reflect the message of the upside-down kingdom that Jesus describes in this section, and verses 11-12 are the end of His thesis.

Even though Jesus wasn't a politician, His message was deeply political (why else do you think they killed him?) If He was a politician today, this would not be the best way to end your thesis. A handler would come out of the shadows to wrangle Jesus in and tell Him to "be positive." But this passage is meant to be positive, it's meant to push those who hear it into living out the rest of Jesus' peculiar message. You see, this passage applies only when you are living out the Beatitudes that come before it! When you work for peace, humble yourself, mourn with those who mourn, show mercy, etc., you are living out the Kingdom here and now!

Unfortunately, this passage has been co-opted today by well-intended Christians as a catch-all passage anytime they feel that they are being persecuted based on their beliefs. It is one thing to believe the Beatitudes are true, but it is something else entirely to believe them and live them out every day. As followers of Jesus, we have the promise of Heaven after we die, but Jesus' Kingdom is also about life today. Once we have been transformed by the message of the Gospel, we have been given the task to live out the Kingdom here and now, and sometimes the church is going to be persecuted for that, and you could be as well! Loving like the Serving King is risky business…

RA

DAY 38

Salt

"No man is worth his salt who is not ready at all times to risk his well-being, to risk his body, to risk his life, in a great cause." —Theodore Roosevelt

You are the salt of the earth, but if salt loses its taste, how shall its saltiness be restored? It is no longer good for anything except to be thrown out and trampled under people's feet. (Matthew 5:13)

I confess there are times, more than I'd like to admit, when the power of salt eludes me. While I understand the power of salt, I equally know its power to be profoundly diminished when in isolation, when left on its own. The single grain of salt seems inconsequential, barely noticeable, even disappearing when thrown onto its target. And I too often read this verse in the singular, as though Jesus were talking to me as an individual rather than to the collective body of Christ. I so often forget He is talking to us, the community of faith, the gathering of God's people.

So comes the profound challenge of Jesus to recognize the plural 'you', the gathering of God's people in mass, numbers large enough to make a difference. Too often, the people of God scatter into the wind, leaving one another as isolated grains of salt, each easily absorbed by a culture delighted for us to simply dissolve into the reigning culture. And, thus, the grand tragedy of salt, individuals 'trampled under people's feet', useless and impotent.

But, oh, the power of salt when it recognizes its need to work in tandem with other grains of salt, each radically committed to a 'great cause', a cause worthy of risking our well-being. You will be tempted to isolate yourself, to merely blend in, absorbed into the dominant culture. And you will imagine that even in isolation, your presence, authentic and real, will radically impact the culture into which you have immersed yourself. But, tragically, salt rarely brings about significant change while working as a single grain. Instead, only when salt finds its peers, those equally transformed by the power of God, does it bring about profound change in the culture at hand. Now is the time to find the other grains of salt and, working together, bring about great change as you love on in the ways of the Serving King…

DM

Exposed!

"One is not exposed to danger who, even when in safety is always on their guard."
—*Publilius Syrus*

"You are the light of the world. A city set on a hill cannot be hidden. Nor do people light a lamp and put it under a basket, but on a stand, it gives light to all in the house." (Matthew 5:14-15)

We have all had the dream. We are standing in a crowded room—maybe a classroom—and the spotlight is on us. We stand there frantically searching for what to say, or at least hoping to recall why we are there in the first place. Faces, familiar and unfamiliar, stare expectantly, apparently anticipating some prepared words of wisdom. But nothing comes to mind. We wake up in a cold sweat, heart racing, and thanking God that it was only a dream. Being in the spotlight is troubling enough when we are prepared. It's sheer terror when all eyes are on us, and we have nothing to offer or say.

When we become followers of Jesus, our lives immediately begin to reflect a way of living that is contrary to the world. Although we seek, in the words of Paul, to "live quietly" and mind our own business as best we can (see I Thess. 4:11-12), living in opposition to the world's core values tends to draw attention. Thanks to the faithfulness of God, the presence of Jesus, and the power of the Holy Spirit, when our counter-cultural faith is noticed, we have no need to panic. We are a "city on a hill," but we're not just any old city. As Christians, we become part of the "City of God." We are representatives—ambassadors—of the ways of Jesus Christ in a world in desperate need of hope, peace, and love.

Though we seek to live out the humility of Christ, we need not fear when we are seen as being in opposition to the world's ways. We simply allow the light of Christ to "give light to the whole house" (Matthew 5:15), and to proclaim His message through us as we exchange our ways for His. These works we do when the spotlight is on us—and even when it's not!—are not our own: they are gifts from the Father (see 5:16). Holiness, then, is not a performance that God expects from us, but, rather, a gift He gives, as we allow His ways to shine through us as we love like the Serving King...

CC

DAY 40

Standing Firm in a Changing World

"Wrong does not cease to be wrong just because the majority share in it."
—*Leo Tolstoy*

"Do not think that I have come to abolish the Law or the Prophets; I have not come to abolish them but to fulfill them. For truly, I say to you, until heaven and earth pass away, not an iota, not a dot, will pass from the Law until all is accomplished. Therefore, whoever relaxes one of the least of these commandments and teaches others to do the same will be called least in the Kingdom of Heaven, but whoever does them and teaches them will be called great in the Kingdom of Heaven." (Matthew 5:17-20)

In today's world, the concepts of "right" and "wrong" have taken on an undeniably arbitrary nature in order to suit the sinful desires of our society. How are we to avoid falling into the trap of believing the lies that the world tells us? Lies such as: If it feels good, do it; or truth is relative. Listen to your heart.

The Bible is very clear on the fallen state of man and teaches that the heart is wicked above all things. To use your heart, as the rudder steering you through life, will only lead to brokenness and pain. Fortunately, for believers, the Big Book found in the back of the pew offers not only the path to salvation, but a roadmap to keep us from traveling down routes that lead to destruction. The commandments in the Bible often clash with what the world claims to be 'right.' However history reveals that for centuries, cultures that embrace the corrupt desires of the world such as lust, greed, and a thirst for power always crumble under the weight of their own sin eventually. We must not forget the warning of Sodom and Gomorrah as our society heads farther and farther down a road that leads away from Biblical Law. Instead, we must hold true to the values we know to be right. We must be deeply-rooted trees, un-swayed by the storms of the world, and, in this, we will find peace. We can rest in the knowledge that we are held to an unshakeable, unchangeable standard, one that does not bend to the whims of the world.

When you find yourself struggling to maintain your morality in our changing world, refresh yourself by reading through the words of Christ in Matthew 5. There are great rewards for those who hold fast to the commands of God and dare to keep loving like the Serving King...
SC

Words Matter

"We have all felt the brazenness of words without emotion, the hollowness, the unaccountable unpersuasiveness of eloquence behind which lies no love."
—Henry Drummond

"You have heard that it was said to the people long ago, 'You shall not murder, and anyone who murders will be subject to judgment.' But I tell you that anyone who is angry with a brother or sister will be subject to judgment. Again, anyone who says to a brother or sister, 'Raca,' is answerable to the court. And anyone who says, 'You fool!' will be in danger of the fire of hell." (Matthew 5:21-22)

It has never been easier to share your thoughts, ideas, and opinions as it is today. Anyone can take out their phone or computer and, in a matter of seconds, speak into a world full of people without qualification of any kind. Anyone can say anything! People have found freedom in word and video form.

While there is power in this freedom to speak into the world, there is also danger. You see, we are responsible for our words and the power that they wield. In the Scripture portion for today, we hear that not only is it sinful to murder, but to call your sister or brother a fool! This is a reality that all need to understand.

We have probably all had times as children when we said, "Sticks and stones may break my bones, but words will never hurt me." While it sounds good, it simply is not true. Words can cut, stab, tear, and kill the heart. Words can leave scars that last a lifetime. Words build up and tear down.

We all have our good days and our bad days. We have all been hurt and made angry. However, we don't have to allow these things to get the better of us. Instead, as Christians, we are called to be forgiving and loving (even when we are angry). Some practical ways to guide you are: Take the time to pray before you speak. Use your words carefully. What are the ramifications of what you say? How will this affect the other person? Important questions for those radically committed to loving like the Serving King...
ME

DAY 42

Work It Out

"Kind words do not cost much. Yet they accomplish much." —Blaise Pascal

"Therefore, if you are offering your gift at the altar and there remember that your brother or sister has something against you, leave your gift there in front of the altar. First go and be reconciled to them; then come and offer your gift.

(Matthew 5:23-24)

There was once a church in which two families were a part. Both had attended church together for years in loving harmony. Then, one day, a disagreement arose between a member of each family. The disagreement went on until one day one family moved to the far right side of the sanctuary. Before long, the disagreement continued to fume, and the second family moved to the far left hand side of the sanctuary. Despite many years of prayer and attempts at reconciliation and revival services, the division continued.

A couple generations came and grew in the church, and along with this time passing, a new pastor came. It didn't take long to realize that there was some sort of issue; although, the pastor couldn't put a finger on it. So the decision was made that he would seek out answers. However, upon asking people from both families, no one could explain what the problem was. They only knew that there had been a disagreement. Although the division remained, the actual issue that had started all the fuss had long been forgotten.

The sad reality is that even within the body of believers we can allow disagreements get the best of us. We say that we don't like confrontation, and decide it is simply easier to allow things to go in hopes that eventually they will work themselves out. The problem is that things rarely just work out. Instead, we are told that when we know someone has a problem with us, we are supposed to go and resolve it.

When we are willing to talk through problems, put our pride aside, and ask forgiveness, amazing things happen. Not only do we avoid years of being noneffective for the Kingdom of God, but we are blessed for doing so. Don't let walls be built around you. Instead, model behavior that is redemptive. You will model correct living and glorify your Father in Heaven. Love on in the ways of the Serving King…
ME

Nip It In The Bud...

"I think it's time for the media and our leaders to get real and start telling the truth about the impact of adultery on our national life." —Mike Pence

"But I say to you, 'Everyone who looks at a woman with lustful intent has already committed adultery with her in his heart.'" (Matthew 5:27)

It is the dilemma that haunts us all, a common thread of experience linking our brokenness into a dangerous web, an opportunity for chaos like no other: Lust. Without a doubt, the mechanism serves a healthy role in human relationships, initiating relationships between the genders, enabling us to overcome what initially appears to insurmountable, the distinct and profound differences between men and women. And we would like to think, once its purpose is served, uniting a man and a woman, we could abandon it, or least turn it off, rendering it void and useless from that point on. Rarely is that ever the case.

To the contrary, lust appears to be an ever-present foe, constantly lurking in the human heart, content to wait patiently, decade after decade if need be, for that opportune moment of weakness. Amazingly, lust seemingly needs so little nourishment to survive. Instead, it's content to wait in hibernation, easily awakened by the first warmth of a new relationship. Thus, the warning of Jesus is some of His severest words in the New Testament.

The uninitiated, those living in the illusion, persuaded the beast can be managed, have long substituted the ethic of the Serving King with a more palatable alternative, "Window shopping never hurts, if you don't go into the store and buy." It is they who play with the beast, confident the chain will hold. Unfortunately, human history is filled with the tales of broken chains. And the cost beyond measure, as the beast ravages those in its path.

So the warning of Jesus to never ever take the beast window shopping. Once allowed to roam the streets, the beast becomes quickly unmanageable, breaking even the strongest of chains. Tame it while it can be tamed. This beast must be nipped in the bud as love on in the ways of the Serving King...
DM

Cut Off What?

"Many kiss the hand they wish cut off." —George Herbert

"If your right hand causes you to sin, cut it off and throw it away. For it is better to lose one of your members than that your whole body go to hell."

(Matthew 5:30)

First, Jesus tells us not to lust, to even contemplate sexual sin. Then, the suggestion to start cutting things off your body, to pluck out your eye or cut off your hand. Is Jesus serious? Is this just a scare tactic, a motivational tool? Is Jesus simply wanting us to realize the gravity (seriousness) of this teaching?

We live in a day, or maybe it has always been this way, where people really do not listen to anything that is uncomfortable or calls for discipline (work). A firm, unyielding understanding of anything (i.e. Lust) is seen as mean-spirited or judgmental. The pervasive attitude seems to be no one has a right to tell me what to do, including God. Even church people struggle to hear anything challenging or convicting. Everything of God is just supposed to be natural, easy, and organic.

We don't talk much about Hell today. It's not comfortable, and, of course, a loving God would never send anybody to Hell. Right? We realize that if we talk about Hell, or cutting things off our body, people will not come to our church. Right? It is our responsibility to make people comfortable and feel good about themselves, like Jesus did, right? But, as we read the Gospels (Matthew- John), we begin to realize Jesus didn't make anyone comfortable, or at least that was not His intention. Jesus lived and taught truth, comfortable or not.

Hell is a real place. If there is a Heaven, logically there must be a Hell. To take the edge off the misery, I usually have people imagine the most pleasurable and ecstatic experiences they could dream of: Heaven. Now, flip that 180 degrees, and you have Hell. Hell will be the most excruciating experience we could ever image, and more. And it is eternal!

Jesus is attempting to help us realize how serious He is about sin, no matter the comfort level or ease. Jesus is letting us know that we have no ability to pull this off on our own. Jesus is telling us there are consequences for not dealing with these issues. But Jesus is letting us know there is hope in His love and grace, but only as we love on in the ways of the Serving King...
JL

Damage Control

"So long as we choose to turn a blind eye to how we are fallen as men or women, and to the unique style of relating that we have forged out of our sin and brokenness, we will continue to do damage to our marriages." —John Eldredge

It was also said, 'Whoever divorces his wife, let him give her a certificate of divorce.' But I say to you that anyone who divorces his wife, except on the ground of unchastity, causes her to commit adultery; and whoever marries a divorced woman commits adultery. (Matthew 5:31-32)

There is an old joke, and you have probably heard it before. It is a joke that is told when someone says something incredibly obvious – so obvious that it really didn't need to be said. When the obvious statement is said, someone else in the group then states, "Besides that Mrs. Lincoln, how did you like the play?" It is simply a light-hearted attempt to demonstrate that everyone already knows what was stated. Sometimes we miss the obvious, when we read the Bible. We are not trying to miss the obvious point, but 2,000 years of history and different cultures can lead us in a different direction. Most people miss the obvious in this famous passage from Matthew 5. We live in a day and time of sexual freedom and questionable morals. We see the Hollywood reports and read stories from the gossip pages. These experiences impact our understanding, so when we read verses 31-32, we think that Jesus is instituting rules that govern divorce.

In the Jewish world of 2,000 years ago, women had very little opportunity and their options were limited. They could not initiate divorce, and they were expected to maintain a proper home. The idea of a married woman having an affair would have been preposterous, but not so with the men. Men had much more opportunity and could divorce their wives for almost any reason. Unfortunately, this was a practice that was rampant. These words of Jesus confront that world. Jesus was not telling the people of that day when it was OK to get a divorce. He was infusing new life and new value into the marriage relationship. In our day, we make a similar mistake. We mistakenly believe the Christian position is that divorce is wrong, so we should avoid it. That is not our position. Our position is that marriage is sacred and holy, and so it should be embraced. We can read Matthew 5 and start to look for reasons to divorce, but we would miss what Jesus was doing. In the midst of this trial, or in the middle of this difficult stretch, what can I do to demonstrate that my home and wife are sacred? That is our real task as we love on in the ways of the Serving King...

DW

Glass Fragments

"Liars are always most disposed to swear." —Vittorio Alfieri

"Again, you have heard that it was said to those of ancient times, 'You shall not swear falsely, but carry out the vows you have made to the Lord.' But I say to you, 'Do not swear at all...'" (Matthew 5:33-37)

The Serving King brings up bits of the Law as fragments of glass, reexamining them, seeing something overlooked and calls us over to see with Him. After awhile, we notice He has made a new window, one projecting a different image than before, beautiful and unexpected. We dream that maybe we fit in this image in a way we did not the previous one.

The compulsion to swear comes from the old image. Sinners, hearts twisted by fear, greed, and selfishness, we value our word as worthless. Others, wary of being abused, demand more from us. We respond by conjuring up deity, hoping to convince the other – and ourselves – of our tale as truth. In a way, we attempt to wear the robe of righteousness, tempting God Himself to strike us down should we be straying from truth in any way.

Yet, stray we have in the very act of swearing. If we are worthy to demand God to judge our words, we are already in a relationship with God. If so, we know He will judge our words and deeds, nudging us in our hearts to be as He wills us. There is no need to call on Him. He will not be showcased as some appraiser to prove a point. Recognizing our position under God, our powerlessness before Him, the thought of invoking Him is pure silliness. Even sillier is the idea we are powerful like the Lord, able to cause calamity on ourselves or loved ones, if we were to stray from truth. In reality, there is nothing we can offer but our word.

In the Kingdom of God, this satisfies. As subjects of the Kingdom, we will speak the truth, painful or not. Our word has worth, as others observe our ways of doing reflect a new way of being. As we live within that new window, the image in which we fit, we begin to act as if we belong. We act with the love of the Serving King, not withholding truth from one seeking it, nor forcing it upon one unwilling. Love as if you belong...

BS

DAY 47

Unfair

"I know the world isn't fair, but why isn't it ever unfair in my favor?"
—*Bill Watterson*

"But if anyone strikes you on the right cheek, turn the other also; and if anyone wants to sue you and take your coat, give your cloak as well; and if anyone forces you to go one mile, go also the second mile." (Matthew 5:38-42)

A child at some point cries out, "That's not fair!" We value the ideal of fairness so early and naturally, it may be universal. This ideal worked its way into justice systems in ancient societies as a means to penalize properly, not too lenient but not too harsh. An ethical means for all to accept judgment.

The mature know the fallacy of fairness, retorting, "Life's not fair." There is inherent inequality – unfairness – in circumstances, abilities, resources, about anything the world values. Applied to justice, fairness can almost never be achieved. We want what we had, not some replacement. Humans extract that extra bit of retribution that satisfies the emotional loss. So God established limits restraining unbridled vengeance.

The Serving King will have none of it. Embracing inequality, He requires a new view of justice, an ethics of empathy and selflessness. He knows justice imitating fairness does not deter evil, only those clumsily pretending. Evil cares not for justice nor punishment but seeks destruction and ruin. Evil will never allow equality while possessing power. Rather than battle on evil's ground, Jesus leads us somewhere better. Dismissing the value placed on worldly concerns, He tells us to give up what has no eternal value, to embrace worldly unfairness.

Instinctively, we rebel against this instruction, expecting misery in conceding what is rightfully ours. Until one day, we realize it is not misery but freedom – freedom from evil's power, freedom to recklessly pursue God's riches – that Jesus is offering. Freedom to forgive, understand, be gentle, and uplifting. Freedom to trade in Holy currency. It dawns on us; we only consider fairness when at a loss. The Serving King's fate was unfair to our advantage. Suddenly, we choose to break the cycle of violation and retribution. As one Canadian parliamentarian of old said, "If we were to go back to…an eye for an eye…very few honorable gentlemen in this House would not be blind." Live unfairly and keep loving…

BS

DAY 48

Radical love

"We must develop and maintain the capacity to forgive. He who is devoid of the power to forgive is devoid of the power to love. There is some good in the worst of us and some evil in the best of us. When we discover this, we are less prone to hate our enemies." —Martin Luther King Jr.

"You have heard that it was said, 'You shall love your neighbor and hate your enemy.' But I say to you, Love your enemies and pray for those who persecute you, so that you may be sons of your Father who is in heaven. For He makes His sun rise on the evil and on the good and sends rain on the just and on the unjust." (Matthew 5:43-45)

Inevitably, those who chase longest after the Serving King soon discover His aptitude for turning life principles upside down. Here comes the shocking challenge to embrace enemies in an upside-down manner, in a spirit of love. Jesus flips the script here. He wants us to love our enemies and not just our friends.

I have discovered how incredibly difficult this challenge can be. But I have equally discovered tools to enable profound changes in my 'default mode' especially when dealing with enemies. For me, it is impossible to hate someone, when I spend time praying for them, seeking the Father's will for them. I suspect Jesus knew as much, so the command to pray for our enemies, the journey down the 'road less traveled'. It can be hard to pray for the well-being of those who curse us, even persecute us. But it is the road to healing and recovery.

Think about who in your life could be counted an enemy. Have you prayed for them today? That is the heart God has for people, and we need to develop more of that heart for people. It begins by adding them to a prayer rotation. As He usually does, Jesus gives us a reason for this type of radical love. Simply put, in the eyes of Jesus, all people are loved the same. He does not divide the world into "us" and "them." He encourages us to love people with that same equity. When the land is dry, He sends rain for all not just the righteous. Evil people can still take advantage of the sun and its benefits, and we ought to share with everyone the love that God has shown us. This is indeed a road less traveled, but a road we should trod on more often, as we love on in the ways of the Serving King…

SV

Perfect love

"Do I not destroy my enemies when I make them my friends?" —Abraham Lincoln

"For if you love those who love you, what reward do you have? Do not even the tax collectors do the same? And if you greet only your brothers, what more are you doing than others? Do not even the Gentiles do the same? You therefore must be perfect, as your heavenly Father is perfect." (Matthew 5:46-48)

The trek after the Serving King often mandates a radical shift from the values that have dominated our lives. Oftentimes, in our world and lives, we only give love to those who love us, or those that can give us some benefit through their love. We are too often pragmatic in our approach to love. Thus, we frequently show love to people that love us, because it is easy, coming naturally to most of us. No surprise, Jesus suggests anyone can love that way, even tax collectors and Gentiles manifest that kind of love.

But here, Jesus calls us to be different, to love people that are difficult, even the unlovable. When it comes to love in the Christian faith, we are called to be counter-cultural, to love the unlovable, those who make love challenging. It is necessary for us to show love to the unlovable, in order to show Christ's love to a world that largely misunderstands love. Jesus ends the passage by saying this type of love is perfect, reflecting the characteristic of His Father.

And as we become more like Christ, we, too, through His grace, can love people with that same perfect love. Today, I am challenged to try and show the world the perfect love of God, to strive to love those who have not earned my love. I am reminded of God's love for me, when I was unlovable, unkind, unworthy of the love God showed me. The perfect love of God casts out fear, even if we are afraid that our love will be rejected or manipulated. Are you wanting to be loved by everyone? Are you thinking that love is only nice and kind? Or are you willing to love those who make it difficult and to not quit? I sense the Serving King leading me down another 'road less travelled' as I love on in His way…
SV

But What Will People Think?

"One of the best ways to deal with the peer pressure of the 'Fear of Missing Out' is to opt-out whenever possible." —Dana Perino

"Beware of practicing your righteousness before other people in order to be seen by them, for then you will have no reward from your Father who is in heaven. Thus, when you give to the needy, sound no trumpet before you, as the hypocrites do in the synagogues and in the streets, that they may be praised by others. Truly, I say to you, they have received their reward. But when you give to the needy, do not let your left hand know what your right hand is doing, so that your giving may be in secret. And your Father who sees in secret will reward you." (Matthew 6:1)

This short phrase alters the actions of more people than we will ever know. In a society where perception often is more important than truth, what people think about a situation normally means more to us than the actual reality of the situation. Peer pressure is a powerful force; it can affect us even in times where the crowd isn't pressuring us into a decision. Sometimes, in our minds, we create an imaginary stage on which we live our lives before an illusionary audience watching our every move. Each act then becomes a performance for those around us, under the notion that they really are paying close attention; when in reality, they are most likely too busy with their own lives to be worrying about mine.

False charity, righteousness, and love done to please the crowd often finds expression in our actions. When performed for the approval of others, the recipients of such acts go from being people loved to people used as props to bolster one's image to others. Nothing can rob a selfless act of its beauty faster than that very act secretly conducted for selfish means. The problem is only the individual performing the act can know their true motivation. When the motivation is for the crowd, we are not just lying to the crowd but manipulating them. However, God knows our true heart. The person to whom we tell the greatest lie is one's self. Break free from the lie and love like the Serving King…
WH

The Show

"Hypocrites in the Church? Yes, and in the lodge and at the home. Don't hunt through the Church for a hypocrite. Go home and look in the mirror. Hypocrites? Yes. See that you make the number one less." —Billy Sunday

"And when you pray, you must not be like the hypocrites. For they love to stand and pray in the synagogues and street corners, that they may be seen by others." (Matthew 6:5-6)

There are two words of significance tied together here I find really interesting. Both evoking imagery relating to face or direction. They are the Hebrew words for pray and hypocrite.

The word for prayer has, at its origin, the idea of face, in the sense of looking toward, beseeching or asking for by looking directly in the person's eyes. The idea here is that we face God and God faces us. There is a reciprocal relationship here that we sometimes lose sight of. That of not only asking God to meet our needs but also to hear from Him. His love for us, His desire for us and, in short, receiving our 'marching orders' for the day, so to speak.

The word used for hypocrite has its origins in the theatre. Think about the symbols often associated with actors. Two masks, one depicting comedy and the other, tragedy. This is the picture of hypocrisy. Actors would hold one mask up to indicate whichever emotion was appropriate. This is what we, as humans, often do. We hold up a mask in front of our face to project what we want the world to see according to the situation. And, much like the actors on the stage who receive applause or a standing ovation, only to take of the mask when the show is over. They have, in essence, received their just reward for putting on a show, a façade, having hidden their true self behind a mask. Acting at its best. There is no more poignant image than the picture of a clown with tears running down his face, the audience long gone home, and he is left alone with his thoughts.

So comes the challenge of the Serving King. Ignore the temptation to 'act out' righteousness before the crowds. Instead, quietly move into the presence of the Serving King. Never lose sight of His eyes as you pray into the night. It is the way of those loving on in the way of the Serving King…

BB

DAY 52

Open Sesame and Other Magic Words

"Prayer is simply talking to God like a friend and should be the easiest thing we do each day." —Joyce Meyer

"And when you pray, do not heap up empty phrases as the Gentiles do, for they think that they will be heard for their many words. Do not be like them, for your Father knows what you need before you ask him." (Matthew 6:7-8)

It's the classic scene in the movie. The hero's path into the cave is blocked. The hero tries everything to get into the cave and finally has a stroke of genius. The hero stands tall, stares down the wall, and says in a deep, authoritative voice those words from the famous Ali Baba and the Forty Thieves, "Open Sesame." To the hero's shock and delight, the magical door opens, and they continue on their journey.

Throughout the ages, humanity has either used God in an attempt to show off their own immense religiosity, or has approached God as if He were a magical door. When in a difficult position, we attempt to say the right words in the right way, or say enough words – hoping maybe we will eventually hit on the magical combination that will open the door and all our needs will suddenly be met. However, to our dismay, God is not a door that can be opened with magical words. He is not a genie to be summoned by the rubbing of a lamp. And He is not a man that can be manipulated into doing our bidding. God is God. He cannot be pushed, pulled, or dragged where you want Him to go… but He can be moved. He will move to act on behalf of His children long before they even ask.

God already knows what we need. He does not need a well-crafted 30-minute speech on why we need it. He knew what we needed long before we ever figured it out. Instead of trying to find the magical combination to unlock the blessings of God, try less words and more you. Approach God as your Good Father instead of some unfamiliar acquaintance that needs to be persuaded to your cause. When we seek a depth of relationship with God rather than seeking that which He could do for us, we find we no longer need many words, and yet, we will be drawn to speak to Him all the more. Love on in the way of the Serving King…

MS

DAY 53

Transformed by a Conversation

"Pray as though everything depended on God. Work as though everything depended on you." —Saint Augustine

Pray then like this: "Our Father in heaven, hallowed be Your name..."

(Matthew 6:9)

Nothing He seemed to be saying made sense to them. He was challenging everything they had ever known to be true. Jesus sat on the hillside seemingly changing all the rules that had guided their lives and society. Over and over, Jesus spoke this phrase, "You have heard that it was said." It was a favored introductory expression that was followed by an earthshaking announcement – a pronouncement that indicated a new reality.

Multiple subjects were covered, and now His attention turned to prayer. In a few simple words, He forever transforms His followers' understanding of prayer. No more repetition or empty phrases. Nor was the focus to be on making God aware of our needs. He already knows what we need before we pray.

No – prayer was to be about a relationship. About expressing, experiencing, and deepening that relationship – "Our Father." It was to be about growing in our understanding of who He is – "who art in heaven." In 52 short words, Jesus changes prayer from useless babblings to a relational conversation with our Father; a refreshing revolution that makes prayer a meaningful conversation that literally transforms who we are, as we experience the presence of the Almighty God when we speak to Him.

As we transcend time and, in our mind's eye, sit at Jesus' feet on the grassy mountainside, His teaching amazes us – even astonishes us. We, who are otherwise individuals of no real account, find ourselves as being viewed by the God and Creator of the universe as one of His children. We get to start a conversation with Him by addressing Him as our Father. Repeating those words causes us to get momentarily sidetracked, as we contemplate the fact that "I am a child of the King."

But the amazement doesn't end there. Jesus' exemplary prayer also reveals that our royal blood flows from no ordinary King. Our Father dwells in Heaven. It's too much! We must pause again in our prayer to soak in whom we are speaking with. Jesus is providing for us a truly transformational prayer.

DS

Character Changes The Conversation

"If you have not chosen the Kingdom of God first, it will in the end make no difference what you have chosen instead." —William Law

"Our Father in heaven, hallowed be Your name. Your kingdom come, Your will be done, on earth as it is in heaven." (Matthew 6:9-10)

You can't judge a book by its cover. And you can't judge the character of an individual by their name either; that is, with one notable exception!

Jesus continues His lesson on prayer by indicating to His disciples that they should acknowledge the special characteristic of God's name – hallowed be Your name. If even God's name is hallowed, certainly God Himself is hallowed. Knowing this quality of His name tells a lot about our Father. We gain incredible insight into His character.

Through this model prayer, Jesus is revealing to us that God's name is set apart from all others, and, like God Himself, it is holy and sacred. He and His name embody everything that is clean, pure, and righteous.

This changes our approach in prayer. We must balance our close relationship with Him - our Father - with His holiness. Like the self-revelation that Peter experienced in Luke 5, this prayer guides us into recognizing how different God is from us.

With this balanced view of God, Jesus then leads His disciples to ask for two things; first, that His Kingdom would come, and second that His will would be done. These insights that Jesus unveils are foundational to our desire to pray for these two suggested requests. When we understand that He is our Father, that He is the God of the heavens, and that He is a righteous, just God, we will long for His Kingdom and obedience to His will. Our hearts understand that the Kingdom of such a God has to be a wonderful thing to experience. We, therefore, long to live in a world where His will would be followed like it is in Heaven.

We are ready to experience such a Kingdom; we are ready to bow before the King of this Kingdom. We know this is the reality in Heaven, and the day is coming when we will experience it there; but we don't want to wait. Our hearts cry out to know it now, and Jesus encourages is to pray for it now. It is the way of loving like the Serving King...
DS

Enough is Enough

"Truth is, I think, if God just gave us our daily bread, many of us would be angry. 'That's all you're going to give me? You're just going to give me enough to sustain me for today? What about tomorrow or next year or 10, 20, 30 years from now? I want to know that I'm set up.' And yet Jesus says just pray for your daily provisions." —Francis Chan

"Give us this day our daily bread..." (Matthew 6:11)

It is just enough. Like Goldilocks, it is just right – not too much, not too little. It meets the need for the day, and that is all we ever really need. If today's needs are met, all our real needs are met.

"Give us this day our daily bread."

The prayer that Jesus teaches us is not the first time God had communicated to His people about focusing on the need for food one day at a time, "Then the Lord said to Moses, "Behold, I am about to rain bread from Heaven for you, and the people shall go out and gather a day's portion every day... Let no one leave any of it over till the morning" (Ex 16:4,19), nor would it be the last...

"So do not worry about tomorrow; for tomorrow will care for itself" (Matthew 6:34).

Once again, Jesus is revealing something extremely important, and, if we are not careful, we will miss it. The key word here unlocking this great spiritual truth is the word "daily." This may not be what we want to hear – God meeting our needs from day to day. We would be much more comfortable if God provided in such a way that assured us that our needs would be met for the rest of our lives. But He knows something about us. As comfortable as such a supply would be, it can lead to us to taking God's provisions for granted, even to a place that we no longer recognize the supply we are experiencing is from God.

The prayer Jesus teaches us draws us back to God, the Great Supplier. When we depend on Him to meet the need of the day, it reminds us that everything comes from Him. When we have abundant resources that can last for many days, even years, we run the risk of forgetting that all of that supply originally came from God. Full stomachs often make loving like the Serving King a relic of the past...

DS

A Cure for Pain

"When you forgive, you in no way change the past - but you sure do change the future." —Bernard Meltzer

"and forgive us our debts, as we also have forgiven our debtors. And lead us not into temptation, but deliver us from evil." (Matthew 6:12-13)

Our pain has a story. It's a story of our past; a story of our sin and the damage that sin causes in our lives and in every other life ours touches. The Good News is our story doesn't end with the pain. This unbearable, unending pain has a solution, a God-provided remedy: "Forgive us our debts, as we also have forgiven our debtors."

Forgiveness. Jesus teaches us to pray for forgiveness. Our pain; our sin has left us with a debt - a moral obligation. A debt we are incapable of paying. "The wages of our sin is death" (Roman 6:23). But we can be forgiven. Our debt can be erased - the obligation removed. However, this is no superficial grace that we are offered. This forgiveness Jesus teaches us to ask for isn't one-sided. He is not calling us to a lifestyle that allows us to demand justice from others who have wronged us while receiving mercy for our offenses. Rather, we are to pray to receive a forgiveness that resembles the type of forgiveness we offer to others. We should be willing to forgive others to the same degree and measure that we want to be forgiven.

Jesus concludes His lesson about pray by encouraging us to pray for protection from temptation – having been forgiven of sin, we do not want to return to sin. It's our first glimpse that there is a different lifestyle possible. His direction gives us great insight. "Lead us not" informs us that temptation is something we can be led toward and ultimately led or kept away from.

So there are two proactive steps that we should pray to the Father to help us with. First, that He would help us not to be led toward temptation. And, second, that He would deliver us from the evil that is presented to us. Jesus' prayer ends on this very practical step that we all need to implement in our lives. If we pray His prayer, it will change our character and our practices as we love like the Serving King…
DS

Forgiveness in the Midst

"Forgiveness says you are given another chance to make a new beginning."
—Desmond Tutu

For if you forgive other people when they sin against you, your heavenly Father will also forgive you. But if you do not forgive others their sins, Your Father will not forgive your sins. (Matthew 6:14-15)

Forgiveness must be important, because this is the second mention of it in this short teaching. It stands to reason, Jesus knew how difficult forgiveness would be. He knew that unforgiveness is a barrier between us and God. We are reminded in Isaiah 59:2, any sin and unforgiveness is a sin, causing God to hide His face and not hear our prayers.

That is a sobering thought, as there may be a fair number of people in our churches, and, perhaps, you and I are some of them, failing to forgive another person. As Jesus is our model, we must take note that He forgave those who put Him on the cross while they imposed His death sentence. He didn't wait until some later date when He had time to process what happened and 'get over it'. He did it in the midst of the pain and the agony of the offense.

That's a bit challenging for me, because I have withheld forgiveness for much less and waited much longer for my own anger and emotions to subside. Jesus says I must forgive, if I expect to be forgiven. But what happens when the one who follows Christ does not forgive? Let's be clear…we may be reading our Bible, praying with and for others, taking communion, and otherwise participating in the fellowship of believers, but if we are knowingly holding onto an offense and not forgiving another person, we are not following Christ. I know I'm meddling, but let's face it, His is the way of forgiveness. If you are following Him, you will forgive.

We have received the ultimate forgiveness when He died on the cross and conquered death! Who are we to play judge no matter what the offense? Do you want to be forgiven? Do the unthinkable. Whether you are currently being offended or wronged, or it has been years since you buried the hatchet deep in your heart, today is the day to forgive! Today is the day to follow Christ and love like the Serving King…
MR

Meatloaf or Else?

"A fast is not a hunger strike. Fasting submits to God's commands. A hunger strike makes God submit to our demands." —Edwin Louis Cole

And when you fast, do not look gloomy like the hypocrites, for they disfigure their faces that their fasting may be seen by others. Truly, I say to you, they have received their reward. But when you fast, anoint your head and wash your face, that your fasting may not be seen by others but by your Father who is in secret. And your Father who sees in secret will reward you. (Matthew 6:16-18)

Growing up Catholic, I seemed to misunderstand the meaning of Lent and fasting. I never read in the Scriptures where God said to give up meatloaf. I never read in the Bible that I had to abstain from eating chicken. What I seemed to miss in the Sunday morning homily was the intent of the fast or abstention of meat. As Jesus was willingly the sacrificial Lamb of God, I was encouraged to sacrifice something from my life demonstrating my desire to draw closer to the Lord, not out of obligation but out of obedience, just as Jesus was obedient, even unto death. I missed the point. Within these three short verses, Jesus is attempting to teach the crowd using fasting as an example of something one could do in order to, you guessed it, draw closer to the Lord. If you choose to fast, do so with the intent that only the Lord will see, not the masses.

The hypocrite will fast but make it a production. He will frown, speak of his hunger pangs, or possibly walk bent over, thus drawing attention to his sacrifice and suffering. "Truly, I say to you, they have received their reward." The Pharisees would use any part of the law and twist it to serve their needs or to benefit them. They were the hypocrites to whom Jesus was speaking. Jesus said to place a bit of oil on your head and wash your face, then the Lord who sees in secret will give you your reward (Matthew 6:17-18). Washing is typically done in private. So, if you choose to fast, maintain a low profile. Gentlemen, whatsoever you do, do with a Godly intent, so the One that sees the intent of your heart (in secret) will reward you in secret, in Heaven! Loving like the Serving King often requires anonymity...
JP

Trash or Treasure

"God has entrusted us with his most precious treasure - people. He asks us to shepherd and mold them into strong disciples, with brave faith and good character." —John Ortberg

"Do not lay up for yourselves treasures on earth, where moth and rust destroy and where thieves break in and steal, but lay up for yourselves treasures in Heaven, where neither moth nor rust destroys and where thieves do not break in and steal." (Matthew 6:19-20)

What do you value? How do you know where you are storing treasure? Take a look at your time. Does your schedule reflect that you value your faith? Is your time spent seeking holiness and Christ-likeness? What about how you spend your money? Do your expenses show that same holiness and Christ-likeness? Often, in western culture, our expenses frequently show a desire to have better things, to be liked, to seek pleasure. What do yours reveal about what you value? Clearly, there are necessary things we must spend both time and money on, things like a place to live, food to eat, and so on. So how do we do that in a way that is seeking heavenly treasure rather than earthly treasure?

We seek heavenly treasure by asking ourselves two questions. First, how does this use of my time and resources influence my world for Christ? This might be as simple as checking if the products you buy are produced with forced labor, or if the food you eat is produced in a way that shows good stewardship to God's creation. It may also be considering if our time is spent in a way that isolates us from others or develops community.

Second, we need to ask ourselves, what is our motivation? Often, this means considering not just individual purchases and uses of our time, but also how our overall schedule and budget are spent. Are we drawn into the culture of consumerism and entertainment, or are we drawn into fellowship with God and one another? Perhaps, this is a note in your wallet reminding you that you are stewards of what God has given to use for His glory. Perhaps, it is an alarm on your phone reminding you to pray for others. Take a moment now to ask God to show you where your treasure is. Ask Him if there is anything that needs to change as you love on like there Serving King…

RS

Where the Heart Is...

"Treasure your relationships, not your possessions." —Anthony Dangelo

"For where your treasure is, there your heart will be also." (Matthew 6:21)

Jesus tells us in this passage that we will find our heart in the place that we are investing ourselves in. To live in this world is to have responsibilities. Jesus knows that we want to provide security, health, and happiness for our family as well as ourselves. This is a God-given human desire. Furthermore, God calls us to faithful work, doing our best in whatever task we are given. With this passage, we may find ourselves feeling like it is impossible to invest in heavenly things with the expectations and responsibilities that are placed on us. God knows this too.

Over and over throughout the Old Testament, Israel is found trusting not God, but a golden calf, a king, a foreign army, a foreign god. They had the same desire for security, health, and happiness, but they forgot that their God was Jehovah Jireh, the Provider. I wonder if we do the same. Do we find ourselves investing in work that does not glorify God, because we think it will provide security? Do we invest ourselves in things and activities that do not glorify God, because they make us feel happy for a moment? Maybe, we find ourselves working at the expense of our health, our families, our faith, because the need for security is so keenly felt. Do we find ourselves, as Israel did, looking to everything around us to provide not only those things we need, but our very identity?

At its root, this passage is not about a list of things we should have or not have, do or not do. It is about trust. Do we trust our Creator to know what we need? Do we hold things loosely, because our security is in Christ, not in things? Do we do our work with joy, because we know our identity is as His children, not in how much we produce? When we daily give our heart to Christ, our treasure will be in Christ too. Those who love in the way of the Serving King abound in treasure that matters...
RS

The Reality Of Seeing

"Are you more devoted to your idea of what Jesus wants than to Himself? If so, you are likely to hear one of His hard sayings that will produce sorrow in you. What Jesus says is hard, it is only easy when it is heard by those who have His disposition."—Oswald Chambers

"The eye is the lamp of the body. So, if your eye is healthy, your whole body will be full of light." (Matthew 6:22)

It is a devastating moment when Jesus broaches the subject of your 'riches', whether it be relationships, dollars, time, etc. Every trekker has riches of one sort or another, some known, but many, if not most, unbeknownst even to the heart's owner. But for those who trek closely after the Serving King, there comes a moment of clarity, a seeing of that which has been buried for a very long time. It is the gift of sight none can avoid, the reality of finally seeing.

Understand, 'sadness' is the typical response to seeing the hard things of life, even one's love of wealth. Jesus warned us "...where your treasure is, there will be your heart also" (Matthew 6:21). It is only in the most profound 'sadness' that the true 'disposition' of the heart reveals itself. There is no other way to peel away the pretenses of 'loving God with all of your heart, mind, and soul.' Disclosure of the heart's secrets is the only way. Only Jesus really knows the 'heart'. Only He can help you to finally see the secrets of the heart, the heart He sees so clearly.

But therein lies the 'surprise' in your question to the Serving King, "What must I do...?" for only Jesus really knows the 'riches' of your heart. The human 'heart' does not reveal its most cherished possessions, even to the owner of the 'heart'. Your sadness comes when Jesus reveals to you what your 'riches' really are. So comes the profound sadness arising out of Jesus' insight into the depth of your heart's desire. This sadness is acute, more so than you have ever experienced. It strikes suddenly and to the very core of your being.

Nonetheless, you are genuinely seeing, finally comprehending, the deepest secrets of the inner being. Light is finally shining brightly in your whole body, your entire being. Only now have you finally discovered how to love in the way of the Serving King. And yes, the light is bursting forth as you chase on after the Serving King...
DM

DAY 62

Yes, Master!

"Well it may be the Devil, And it may be the Lord, But you're gonna have to serve somebody" —Bob Dylan

"No one can serve two masters, for either he will hate the one and love the other, or he will be devoted to the one and despise the other. You cannot serve God and money." (Matthew 6:24)

Bob Dylan's lyrics are a modern version of Jesus' words in Matthew's Gospel. Dylan's words delineate the range of roles that we could play in our 21st century world. He points out that whatever your role in life, you will always be serving somebody, the Lord or the Devil. Abraham Lincoln, on June 16, 1858 in Springfield, while running for the Senate, said "A house divided against itself cannot stand…. this government cannot endure half slave and half free." Our lives also cannot be divided in our loyalties. The Greek word Jesus used for 'serve' (douleou) and 'slave' (doulos) are from the same root word. We are bound as a slave.

Whatever the driving motivation for your life may be, it will become your "Master." Concert pianist Stephen Hough, on his twitter feed, stated that he generally managed about four hours of practice per day. In just 10 years, he will have spent 25% of his waking hours sitting at the piano keyboard just practicing. It could be said that he is a slave to his talent in much of his life.

In Western culture today, we are immersed in a materialistic world. It creates an insatiable drive to make more money to buy more and more things. Reality shows, shopping networks, travel programs, and even network news commercials create desire for whatever they promote. It is clear that this onslaught overwhelms all other priorities in our lives.

As we become enslaved to our appetites, we focus upon the material and are distracted from the more important and the spiritual elements of our lives. We must consciously oppose these forces of our culture to have more time for our children, our spouse, and friends. Each one must examine the activities of our lives. How much time do we spend with our families? What activities enhance our lives? How much time is wasted on non-productive activities? How much time do we spend focused upon God and living our lives as Jesus would in our situations? Ultimately, we must decide…whom will we serve? Love on…
DS

Soil Of The Soul

"A warning which needs to be reiterated is that the cares of this world, the deceitfulness of riches, and the lust of other things entering in, will choke all that God puts in. We are never free from the recurring tides of this encroachment."
—*Oswald Chambers*

"Therefore I tell you, do not be anxious about your life, what you will eat or what you will drink, nor about your body, what will you put on. Is not life more than food, and the body more than clothing?" (Matthew 6:25)

The relentless 'encroachment' of the cares of this life find power, not in an overwhelming assault upon our deepest needs, but, rather, a perpetual chipping, one that is rarely felt, painlessly eroding the 'soil' in which the character of God is desperately trying to take root deep within your being. They do not assault the character of God directly, clearly a waste of time, for the character of God established in you cannot be eroded. No, the relentless assault is upon the 'soil of the soul' in which the character of God is attempting to sink deep in life-changing roots.

Nor are the relentless waves 'bad' or 'evil', in and of themselves. To the contrary, these ever-pounding waves of desire are the very 'desires' and 'wants' God planted deep within you, but they are 'rogue waves' amplified by a steady and relentless pounding from the culture around you which feeds and thrives on your dependence upon 'things' rather than God as the source of contentment and peace.

Tragically, the 'tides of encroachment' do not lessen with each passing day; instead, they crash upon the 'soil of the soul' in each and every moment of life. The child of God will have to learn those vital 'erosion protection techniques' that replenish the 'soil of soul' on a daily basis. Erosion will occur. Protection will never be enough; replacement must happen. The child of God will have to find those 'erosion buffets', and this will not be easy, for the terrain of the soil is different for each one trekking after the Serving King. You will be tempted to mimic the 'erosion prevention techniques' that others have found powerful and effective. In the end, no two soils are ever the same; hence, nor can be the techniques that replenish and protect that precious 'soil of the soul'. Are you protecting the 'soil of the soul' as you trek on? Love on in the way of the Serving King…
DM

Cart Before The Horse

"You never have time to do everything, but you always have time to do the important things." —Howard Hendricks

"But if God so clothes the grass of the field, which today is alive and tomorrow is thrown into the oven, will He not much more clothe you, O you of little faith?"
(Matthew 6:30)

Our Men's Study Group at Nampa College Church has been studying the 'Tender Commandments'. As we began to work through them, it became increasingly clear that the first three commandments were not placed there by accident. Placing God or His Kingdom first in your life is critical to the enjoyment of the fullness of the life He has given us. He understands and knows what is best for His creation, and includes your life and mine. Jesus adds a significant element. We are not just seeking God in some mystical way. Seeking God includes the discovery of the characteristics of His nature of essence. The part Jesus points to is His (God's) righteousness. Seeking God is not intended to be a mystical experience of the presence of God alone. It is a union of the seeker with the essence of God Himself. Here, Jesus is emphasizing one aspect of God's nature: Righteousness. In a similar way, Jesus emphasizes God's righteousness as He begins the Lord's Prayer, "Our Father who art in Heaven. Hallowed be thy name." God and righteousness or holiness are again linked together.

In this passage, Jesus also states a result of seeking God… "all these things will be added to you." If you look at this statement, it can almost seem that this is a carte blanche invitation to ask for anything you might desire, and God will give it to you. However, as with other passages on prayer found in Scripture, you must keep the context in mind as you begin to understand what is being said. The clear reference here is back to verses 31 of this chapter. In essence, our basic needs will be met daily, just as God meets the needs of the animals of His creation. Adam Clark states that the early Church Fathers quote, as the words of Christ, "Ask great things, and little things shall be added unto you; ask heavenly things, and earthly things shall be added unto you." Have you come to the place where you can focus upon the things of the Kingdom of God, or is your focus upon the material things the world emphasizes?

Trust God to provide all that you need for life as you dare to love on in the way of the Serving King…
DS

The Sheathed Sword

"There is no getting away from the penetration of Jesus. If I see the mote in your eye, it means I have a beam in my own. Every wrong thing that I see in you, God locates in me. Every time I judge, I condemn myself. Stop having a measuring rod for other people. There is always one fact more in every man's case about which we know nothing." —Oswald Chambers

"Judge not, that you be not judged. For with the judgment you pronounce you will be judged, and with the measure you use it will be measured to you."

(Matthew 7:1)

The problem with the 'measuring rod', and it is a major drawback to every 'measuring rod', is its reflective mirroring affect for those foolish enough to use one; and you will be tempted, rest assured. 'Judging', for better and worse, is innate to the human condition, and the infusion of 'grace' into the human condition strikes at the root of this divine attribute gone horribly wrong through the infection of sin and the consequent distortions to human nature, even within the child trekking after the Serving King. The Divine response to this 'infection' is not to 'improve' or 'heal' this bent in the human condition; rather, to 'ban' the exercise of judgment altogether, "Judge not."

However, the 'judging mechanism', deeply rooted in the human condition, is difficult to reign in, to 'holster' and to render dormant. Thus, Jesus warns those unable to subdue the 'addiction to judge', with its persistent clamoring to be released from the subconscious cell to which the Spirit has banned it, that upon its release it will not fulfill its promise to 'condemn' only those worthy of its wrath. Rather, it will do what it has always done; judge the one who released it from its imprisonment. So, Jesus warns those tempted to release the beast, to stand down, for upon 'judgment's release' what it will search out is not the 'mote in the eye of the other', but, instead, the "...beam in my own."

'Judgment' will whisper continually in your ear, "I am here to help, to merely point out that which needs to be fixed in both the 'other', as well as thine own eye." But you must resist the 'common sense' pleas of 'judgment'. It has no intention of fixing what it sees. No, 'judgment' is a dangerous sword, wielded to wound and maim all who fall under its watchful eye. Only God dare unsheathe this sword. Every child must carry this sword, but none should fall prey to its use. Trek on with this sword sheathed at all times. It is the way of loving in His way...
DM

Blessings Are Not Exclusive

"Rejection just motivates me to keep trying and to try to do better." —*Sasha Grey*

"Do not give dogs what is holy, and do not throw your pearls before pigs, lest they trample them underfoot and turn and attack you." (Matthew 7:6)

Have you ever tried to share your faith and been ridiculed and judged? And when it's happened to me, especially if I didn't wait for the Holy Spirit to tell me where to share, the consequences were uncomfortable, sometimes even painful! Revelations given by God are holy, pearls of great price. But not all are prepared to listen. Jesus warns us that we must be discerning about how and where we share our witness.

The Jews were known as a holy people set apart by and for God. They were very proud of that fact. Jesus took it a giant step farther and declared that all who followed Him were set apart, holy and precious. This revelation was not particularly acceptable to the powerful religious leaders of the time. They judged the rest of the world as unworthy and resented Jesus adding them into what they considered their exclusive blessing.

In this verse, Jesus admonishes the religious leaders, comparing them to culturally-despised dogs and pigs. This was a massive insult. Dogs were considered evil scavengers, unattractive and lowly. Pigs and swine were unclean, dirty, and would literally eat and trample anything. Both were known to turn violent and attack. These were no cuddly pets; to the contrary, these were wild animals. Jesus warned that holy revelations should not be entrusted to people who are unwilling to hear, those whose only intent is to ridicule, find fault, and judge. He cautions that if an attempt is made to share the holy revelations of God with those who reject them, they may mistreat the messenger, turn on him, and find fault with both the message and his faith. Loving like the Serving King can be risky business…
PG

The Silent God Of Random...

"Keep the notion of the mind of God behind all things strong and growing. Nothing happens in any particular unless God's will is behind it, therefore you can rest in perfect confidence in Him." —Oswald Chambers

"...how much more will your Father Who is in Heaven give good things to those who ask Him!" (Matthew 7:11)

It is the 'particulars', those bothersome details of life, often unpleasant and pesky when robbed of meaning and purpose, eroding one's confidence in trekking after the Serving King. You will be tempted to think, "There is no 'mind' or reason to the 'chaos' of events that seem to unfold in the 'particulars' of my life." But such is never, yes never, the case. To the contrary, it is the ability to sense the 'mind of God behind all things', redeeming and purposeful, which sustains and encourages. Yes, the mind of God is indeed behind all things, infusing the seeming 'chaos' with meaning and purpose. 'Random' is an illusion creating despair for those who fail to comprehend the 'mind of God'. And, how the evil one delights in your degradation of the 'mind of God', hidden and mysterious into 'random', that bastion of the foolish (Romans 1:17).

Despair, the companion of 'mindless chaos', that erratic unfolding of common chance events, far removed from the redeeming 'hand of God', orchestrated by the 'mind of God', cripples the child trekking after the Serving King. Once 'crippled', robbed of the ability to trust the 'mind of God', 'asking Him' fades into a jaded memory, void of power, rendering the 'mind of God' nonexistent, replaced by an ever-growing cycle of 'despair' at the feet of 'random'. 'Ask Him' becomes a mere shadow of conversations long dead, long abandoned, surrendered to the 'silent god of random'.

Then the redeeming, reminding, re-powering words of Jesus, "...ask Him." It is our 'perfect confidence in Him', an utter assurance the 'mind of God' is indeed the will behind the particulars, that heals and restores. And no, you will not be given insight as to 'how' the particulars "...work together for the good of those who love God" (Romans 8:28). Yours is the reassurance "...your Father who is in Heaven gives good things to those who ask Him." Strike a death blow to the 'silent god of random'. Dare to ask as Him as you love on like the Serving King...
DM

DAY 68

The Prayer For Good...

"Prayer with most of us is turned into pious platitude, it is a matter of emotion, mystical communion with God. Spiritually we are all good at producing fogs... It is no use praying unless we are living as children of God. Then, Jesus says — 'Everyone that asketh receiveth.'" —Oswald Chambers

"Or which one of you, if his son asks him for bread, will give him a stone?"

(Matthew 7:9)

Those trekking after the Serving King are quick to master the 'art' of asking for 'this or that' with the cacophony of the many, having left behind the hard work of praying in that 'secret place' as Jesus mandated (Matthew 6:6), producing this 'fog' that obscures genuine discourse with God. And the 'fog', rising up out of a lack of comprehension concerning God's ways of being and doing, lingers, making future conversations difficult. Rather than genuine discourse, conversation becomes a parley, that bantering between opposing sides, seeking to find a common ground in which peace and authentic communication can take place. But the parties parleying soon discover they have very different agendas. The trekker, consumed in the early days of the trek with 'What I need', while the Serving King's focus centers upon providing 'what is good'. And the two are very different at times.

The key is to understand the critical nature of the "...know how to give good gifts to your children" (Matthew 7:10). Children, perhaps all children, have to be taught what is good for them. And therein lies the problem. The trekker, lacking knowledge of 'what is good' continues to petition for what is 'needed' as perceived from the limited perspective of one engaged in the trek. Confusion, the by-product of the 'fog', arises when those perceived needs are not met; especially when needs appear to be authentic and immanent. But 'need' and good are two very different entities. And so, with every passing moment, the 'fog' intensifies, making all future dialogue even more difficult.

The secret to the 'fog' dissipating is child's play. Stop asking for 'this or that'. It is only in the quietness of the secret place that the good can be heard. And those trekkers who know the good to ask for, suddenly discover that the good has been flowing for a very long time. It is in that moment of understanding that you begin to understand the good has been gushing toward you all along as you dared to love like the Serving King...

DM

The Golden Rule

"Do unto other, as you would have them do unto you" —The Golden Rule

"So, whatever you wish that others would do to you, do also to them, for this is the Law and the Prophets." (Matt 7:12)

One day, we were unloading a donation of canned food in front of a homeless shelter. Across the street stood a tall, dark gentleman in a trench coat, matted hair, who had always been a bit scary to me. He was carefully watching me unload the food.

I knew he struggled with mental health problems, and, normally, I would have been hesitant, never taking my eye off of him, even to unload the truck. With all my experience being around the homeless, I knew he was really sick, dangerous even, and I should have taken more precautions by having another person with me.

Gently, I heard the Holy Spirit prompt me and say, "He's hungry." Quickly, without hesitation or fear, a new course of action was unleashed. Before he might turn and walk away, I looked for cans with flip lids, easily opened, allowing him to have a meal. Finding a small box, I waved at him to come over. Shell-shocked by life, he just stood there looking at me. I waved again, several times, and invited him to come over. Finally, I held up the box and pointed, suggesting it was for him. Wounded many times in days gone by, he paused and waited, too cautious to move forward. I said, "Are you hungry? Come take this, it's for you!"

Suddenly, as if he was pushed, he quickly came across the street, looked at me, and took the box. Towering over me, he looked above my head, and like he had seen a ghost, he ran away down the street. I often wonder what he saw, or thought he saw, initiating his quick getaway.

To this day, I don't know what frightened him. But when the Holy Spirit prompts you to treat others as Jesus would treat them, even when it seems a bit precarious, walk in wisdom, and treat them as Jesus would treat you. That is the way of loving like the Serving King…

SB

Focused

Productivity is never an accident. It is always the result of a commitment to excellence, intelligent planning, and focused effort. —Paul J. Meyer

"For the gate is narrow and the way is hard that leads to life, and those who find it are few." (Matthew 7:14)

"Stop kidding around," the doctor said, during the eye exam portion of my annual physical. I was nearly 38 years old and had never worn glasses. But this particular morning, as I covered my right eye, even the bigger letters near the top of the eye chart were blurry. I insisted I wasn't joking, and after I washed out my eyes, I tried again. All was still blurry. "You're going to need to go see the eye doctor immediately! Your vision in that eye is pretty bad," the doctor said. From then on, I have worn glasses.

When Jesus speaks of the "narrow way" in Matthew 7:13-14, His words are often viewed in a negative light. However, Jesus' words are not about being limited in our thinking or in our conversations with others. Nor are they meant to imply that Christians should live in some sort of denial of truth, unwilling or unable to explore a variety of options. Rather, this statement from Jesus is about focus.

Jesus reminds all who will follow Him that there are many paths before us to choose from. Also, there are many distractions that seek to keep us from honing in on the path to which God calls us—a path that leads to eternal joy and peace. A frequent analogy Jesus gives about our inability to see His path and follow it is spiritual blindness. How do we keep from being led astray? According to Jesus, we are to narrow our focus. We are to allow God's Spirit to lead us in such a way that His ways move to the foreground and everything else fades. It is by allowing God's ways—as expressed in the life and work of Jesus Christ and the leadership of the Holy Spirit—to become our full focus that we are able to walk in the fullness of all that God has in store. His Spirit becomes our corrective lenses, allowing us to see His way of being and doing more clearly. And so, the challenge to walk in His way as we love like the Serving King…!

CC

One of These Things is Not Like the Others

"Thank you, horseradish, for being neither a radish nor a horse. What you are is a liar food." – Jimmy Fallon

"Beware of false prophets, who come to you in sheep's clothing but inwardly are ravenous wolves." (Matthew 7:15-20)

It was a cold snowy day, when I entered the coffee shop. It was full of comfy, overstuffed furniture and elegant coffee tables on which to place your steaming beverage. The setting tempted you to sit down and put your feet up. On the far wall, a fireplace was blazing. I sat close trying to warm up. The noise of the fire was a soothing lullaby for a busy morning. After sitting for awhile, I noticed I was warming up, but not nearly as fast as I should be. Upon closer inspection of the fire, I found it to be cold. That is correct, fire… cold! I wondered how this could be. I could clearly see the fire. I could even hear the fire, but there was no heat. Then I spotted what I had previously overlooked in my pursuit of comfort. I saw a power cord coming out the back of the 'fireplace' along with little buttons on front. One button read "volume" and another read "channel." I was not sitting in front of a warm fire at all but, instead, sitting like a fool in front of a TV.

It is easy to miss the truth when something is being dressed up and disguised to look like something it's not. This is especially true when what is disguised is pleasing to our desires. Since before Jesus came on the scene, false prophets have infiltrated God's people. The confusion they bring can destroy the community within a group of believers and cause believers to fall away. As children of God, we want to believe the best in everyone (and that is an admirable trait). However, we cannot forget that our enemy, Satan, is intelligent and always looking for ways to bring destruction. With stakes being so high, it is important to be on guard against those who look like children of God but, in reality, want only to destroy us, our brothers or sisters. Jesus reminds us we will know these false prophets by the fruit that they produce. No false prophet loves like the Serving King…

MS

Trees and Fruit

"Sin, guilt, neurosis; they are one and the same, the fruit of the tree of knowledge."
– Henry Miller

"Are grapes gathered from thorn bushes, or figs from thistles? So, every healthy tree bears good fruit, but the diseased tree bears bad fruit. . . Thus you will recognize them by their fruits." (Matthew 7:15-20)

It always seems to come back to trees. In Genesis 3, we are taught about two important trees with two very different kinds of fruit: the Tree of Life and the Tree of the Knowledge of Good and Evil. Adam and Eve were permitted to eat the fruit from any of the trees including the Tree of Life, but they were not to eat from the Tree of the Knowledge of Good and Evil. Adam and Eve disobeyed God and ate from that forbidden tree. As soon as that illicit fruit flavored their tongues and travelled into their bodies, it became known. What is the it to which I refer and to which God sought to keep them from?... sin! Sin immediately entered the world. Sin's violent puncture into our world brought with it hate, corruption, and evil of all kinds.

God cast Adam and Eve out of the garden, so they would no longer be permitted to eat from the Tree of Life. The fruit from the Tree of Life was life eternal and would have allowed Adam and Eve to live forever in paradise and in intimacy with Creator God. The destruction caused by the choice of Adam and Eve to eat from the wrong tree meant that Jesus had to die on a different kind of tree. His death on that 'tree', known as the cross, restores our lives, giving each of us victory over Satan, sin, and death, if we so choose.

A tree cannot hide its true nature and condition. The proof of its state of being literally hangs from its limbs. While many of us often criticize the failure of Adam and Eve, the truth is that God gives each of us the same choice they had. We can choose life through Jesus, or we can choose knowledge of good and evil . . . and death as a result. Our choice will bear fruit in our lives, and it will be obvious to all who care to look deeper what our choice has been. What will your choice be - love and life, or hate and destruction? There cannot be a compromise between the two – it's impossible. It is as impossible as an apple tree producing cacti for fruit. The fruit of loving in His way is easy to distinguish...
MS

Are You Sure?

"What is a 'false prophet'? Those who lie by attributing personal biases to divine source." —Leland Lewis

On that day many will say to me, 'Lord, Lord, did we not prophesy in Your name, and cast out demons in Your name, and do many deeds of power in your name?' Then I will declare to them, 'I never knew you; go away from Me, you evildoers.' (Matthew 7:21-23)

We are living in interesting times. Unlike any time previously, we are bombarded with messages every day. Formerly, one needed access to a media source in order to get their message out, but, today, all one needs is a social media account. There are many people competing for our attention, and many of them claim inside knowledge, or that they are uniquely representative of God. If we will send them $50, we will get a prayer cloth. If we have enough faith, we will be healed from any disease.

Here is a promise and a warning that are given together. There is a promise. Those who do God's will are part of the Kingdom. That seems simple enough, except that all of the people described in this passage claim to be doing God's will. There are those that prophesied and did impressive acts, and all claimed to be aligned with God. Here is the problem. Jesus states that many of these people are not acting for God at all, even while they claim to be doing so. How are we to discern the authentic from the charlatan, those who use God to accomplish his or her own end?

There is much at stake here. One of the Ten Commandments is often translated "do not take the name of the Lord in vain." A better translation would be "do not falsely carry the name of the Lord." When we claim God's leading or involvement when it is not there, we place ourselves in some jeopardy. Yet, we are still faced with the dilemma of properly discerning the authentic from the fake. Here are a few litmus tests for a believer navigating this new landscape: Does the activity bring fame, glory to God, or a person? Does the action divide or bring people together? Does the person exhibit grace or a harsh tone? Does the person speak kindly of other believers, or is this person the only one? Does his/her life exhibit grace, peace, gentleness, kindness, and self-control?

We live in a world that suffers from a lack of authenticity. Unfortunately, this trait has leaked into the church as well. If our lives exhibit authenticity, it will be easier for us to spot what is false as we love like the Serving King...

DW

DAY 74

Straight and Strong Will Always Stand!

"It is not the beauty of a building you should look at; its the construction of the foundation that will stand the test of time." —David Allan Coe

"Everyone who hears these words of Mine and does them will be like a wise man who built his on the rock. And the rain fell, and the floods came, and the winds blew and beat on that house, but it did not fall…" (Matthew 7:24-27)

In Istanbul, Turkey, the foundation of an apartment building was washed away by torrential rains, and the building literally slid off the side of a hill into the building next to it, destroying both. This is exactly what Jesus Christ is warning us of; unless the spiritual-emotional foundation of our lives is strong, straight, and solid, it will never stand the stress.

Jesus focuses on two important aspects of building a rock-solid foundation: First, we are to listen to His teachings. Do we really listen to His teaching (words), or do we listen without listening? It is interesting to ask church attenders what the sermon topic was as they exit the church. Too many tell me they can't remember the topic, but it was good. Sadly, that has become a common practice in our society, since we are bombarded with so much information.

Jesus' second call was for us to 'practice' what we have heard. As the infamous Allen Iverson communicated, "Practice, are we actually talking about practice?" Yes, we are talking about practice. Developing a vision of what we want to accomplish or be, breaking it down in doable steps, and doing it over and over until it becomes natural. Arguably, the greatest basketball player of all time, Michael Jordan; if he were to miss an important free-throw, would take 500 practice shots after the game. He is an example of excellence worth following- in basketball. The adage, practice makes perfect, may be a little exaggerated, but there is truth in it. The more we practice, the more it becomes natural. After enough practice, we don't even think about it. The more we practice the teachings of Christ, they just become natural, and we don't even have to think about them. We just do them, because that is who we have become.

Jesus is right; if we do not listen to His words, and practice them, when the storms of life descend on us, and they will, our soul (mind and heart) will fail. Our lives will fall apart, and we will not know what to do. But if we learn and practice loving like the Serving King, our house will stand strong…

JL

Something Different

"Always, everywhere God is present, and always He seeks to discover Himself to each one." —A. W. Tozer

When Jesus had finished saying these things, the crowds were amazed at His teaching, because He taught as one who had authority, and not as their teachers of the law. (Matthew 7:28-29)

Jesus turned the biblical world upside down. His teaching was different than anything that the people had seen before. While Jesus taught about God and His expectations, He also taught about God's love. This changed everything, and the teachers of the law didn't like it.

These teachers of the law had studied the laws from an early age. They focused on the rules and held them unsparingly. In turn, they also used the laws for their own gain. While they held tight to the laws, they hadn't been changed by God. The rules became more important than the One who had made them and the reasons behind them.

In contrast, Jesus did everything in love. He touched those who were viewed as untouchable. He healed those who others walked right past. He walked into places that others saw as unfit. Jesus stood up for those who were caught in sin, while forgiving them and telling them to go and sin no more. His message was different. He taught the truth, but He did so in love while forgiving sin. He gave hope to those who were lost and broken. Much-needed hope to those who others cast out.

As we live our lives each day, may we remember the stark difference between the teachers of the law and teachings of Christ. May we see those who others choose to overlook. May we not be afraid to touch what others say is unclean. May we bring healing and redemption through Christ Jesus to those who, without Him, are beyond all hope. Instead, will you show the love and gentleness of Christ Jesus to the ones who need to see Him? May we truly do unto others as we would have them do unto us. That is the way of loving like the Serving King...
ME

DAY 76

Danger

"You take the front line when there is danger. Then people will appreciate your leadership." —Nelson Mandela

When Jesus had come down from the mountain, great crowds followed Him; and there was a leper who came to Him and knelt before Him, saying, "Lord, if You choose, You can make me clean." He stretched out His hand and touched him, saying, "I do choose. Be made clean!" Immediately his leprosy was cleansed. (Matthew 8:1-3)

After three chapters of Jesus' teachings, the Gospel of Matthew transitions into Jesus' miraculous act; and the first one is the healing of a man with leprosy. "Leprosy" was a catch-all term for a variety of skin diseases, so we don't know exactly which one this man had, but we do know that any skin disease was enough for him to be cast out of society. These skin diseases were understood to be highly contagious, so anyone showing signs of "leprosy" were forced to live outside the city and to shout that they were "unclean" any time they came near other people.

In this story, the man was breaking the law by approaching Jesus, and we must imagine as he knelt at the feet of Jesus, everyone in the crowd recoiled in fear that he might touch them and give them the disease. Yet, Jesus did not flinch—He didn't seem to react at all to the danger that the man represented. Instead, He invited the man to speak.

When the man spoke, he spoke in words of faith. He knew Jesus could heal him, if only the Lord would choose to do so. The man recognized the power of Jesus, but he wasn't sure about the heart of Jesus. Would Jesus choose him in spite of his disease-ridden, unclean body? Would Jesus put His own health and social status on the line for the sake of this man who had nothing to offer?

When Jesus reached out and touched the man, He did more than heal his body—He restored his dignity and showed us where our hearts should also be. On the heels of teaching on the mountainside (explaining how to love others), Jesus reaches out and touches a man who probably hadn't felt a human touch in years (demonstrating how to love others).

In this story, if we look to the man with leprosy, we learn that God cares about us even in our darkest, most broken moments. If we look to Jesus, we learn that we are to be present with the people society has rejected, even when it risks harm to ourselves. It is the way of love…
RG

DAY 77

Testimony

> *"Share the Gospel at all times. If necessary, use words."*
> —*attributed to St. Francis of Assisi*

Then Jesus said to him, "See that you say nothing to anyone; but go, show yourself to the priest, and offer the gift that Moses commanded, as a testimony to them." (Matthew 8:4)

For the man with leprosy to be able to return to society, being healed wasn't enough—he needed to prove that he was no longer sick. Mosaic law demanded that a priest examine him, declare him clean, and give an offering on his behalf. Following that, he needed to go through more than a week of ritual cleansing (see Leviticus 14). After all that, if the leprosy was still gone, he could re-integrate himself into normal life in the city.

What's interesting about Jesus' command here is that He told the man to go to the priest. Usually, a person in this situation would send for a priest to come outside the city to inspect them and declare them clean. Otherwise, the leprous person would risk spreading the disease to the whole city. But Jesus told the man to go into the city, into the Temple, and present himself the priest. Why would he do that?

We might think that this was a simple act of faith, as the man was undoubtedly healed, but that would have still been breaking Jewish law. Or, it could have been an act of evangelism where the man was to proclaim the testimony of what had happened to him, similar to the preaching of the woman at the well. But here, Jesus asked the man with leprosy to "say nothing to anyone."

Perhaps, though, Jesus was suggesting a different kind of evangelism for this particular situation. The man wasn't supposed to be in the city at all, so maybe Jesus didn't want him to draw undue attention to himself, but, instead, wanted the man to let his example speak a quiet testimony to the healing power and love of God. Rather than calling him to be a street-corner preacher, maybe Jesus was calling him to gently subvert the social standards of exclusion, full of the knowledge that Jesus had made him clean.

Are there places in your life, perhaps, at your workplace or among a certain group of friends, where it might be a mistake to loudly proclaim the Gospel? In those situations, how can you live out your experience of the Gospel in a way that shows the heart of Jesus without using words? How will you employ the silent power of love?

RG

Humility from an Unexpected Source

"The key to successful leadership today is influence, not authority."
—Ken Blanchard

For I too am a man under authority, with soldiers under me. And I say to one, 'Go,' and he goes, and to another, 'Come,' and he comes, and to my servant, 'Do this,' and he does it." When Jesus heard this, He marveled and said to those who followed Him, "Truly, I tell you, with no one in Israel have I found such faith.
(Matthew 8:5-13)

In this encounter with Christ, we find a desperate Roman centurion seeking, finding, and then pleading with Christ to come heal his servant. Interestingly, the word used for 'servant' can also mean 'child'. It's possible this man's child was sick, explaining his utter desperation. When explaining to Christ that he is a man of authority able to tell his soldiers to come and go, he suggests he can also tell his 'servant' to do things. This time, the word for 'servant' can only mean slave. Hence, the desperation of a dad's heart.

He could have easily sent a servant or soldier to go find Jesus and make this request. But, in this case, he comes to Jesus and personally makes a passionate request. This man, a Roman, with great authority over Jesus, a Jew, didn't view Jesus as a subordinate. He didn't even view Jesus as an equal, claiming he did not deserve the presence of Christ under his roof. According to the law at this time, a Roman could force a Jew to carry something for him up to a mile, where he could then set it down, and the Roman could find another Jew to carry it the next mile. For this man to publicly seek out Christ and publicly lower himself when the cultural status said otherwise, demonstrated great faith on two fronts. First, confidence Jesus could perform the healing; and second, the faith to endure certain public scrutiny because of his treatment of Jesus.

There are times in our lives when publicly seeking Christ will lead to public scrutiny. Likewise, there are times when extending the love of Christ to those outside the parameters of the social norms can also generate negative public scrutiny. There is little doubt Jesus Himself may have received some scoffing among His Jewish counterparts at the idea that He would publicly praise this Roman's faith above those He had encountered in Israel. It takes great faith to love like Christ. Love like His almost always comes with a cost...
WH

Faith From An Unexpected Source

"Ability hits the mark where presumption overshoots and diffidence falls short."
—*Golda Meir*

"I tell you, many will come from east and west and recline at table with Abraham, Isaac, and Jacob in the Kingdom of Heaven, while the sons of the kingdom will be thrown into the outer darkness. In that place there will be weeping and gnashing of teeth." And to the centurion Jesus said, "Go; let it be done for you as you have believed." And the servant was healed at that very moment." (Matthew 8:11-13)

The special encounter between Jesus and a Roman Centurion who humbled himself enough as a Roman to come to Jesus (a Jew under Roman occupation) to request He heal a significant person in his life, introduced the reality of "…many will come from the east and west." Such is the way of community in the Kingdom of God.

The reaction Jesus displays is very interesting. He expresses surprise in not finding anyone in Israel with such great faith. Jesus' proclamation does not speak of Israel geographically, but as a people. It must certainly be moving to Him that a non-Jew would place so much faith in Him. Jesus goes on to make a chilling proclamation regarding the fate of so-called 'insiders' of the Kingdom of Heaven. Many will come and presumptively take their places in the Kingdom of Heaven only to be cast out. Scholars often see this as a warning to the Jews to not simply assume their place in Heaven is secure.

I would extend His warning to all of us. Resist the temptation to treat salvation as a given, enabling us to live out our faith carelessly. Further, simply assuming others will not be welcome in the Kingdom of Heaven is equally misleading. At the end of the day, our calling is not to figure out who is in and out of Heaven. Our challenge is to share the love of the Serving King with anyone we encounter. Never be surprised by those who come seeking Jesus. Instead, keep loving like the Serving King…
WH

The Touch of the Master's Hand...

"Optimism is the faith that leads to achievement. Nothing can be done without hope and confidence." —Helen Keller

And when Jesus entered Peter's house, He saw his mother-in-law lying sick with a fever. He touched her hand, and the fever left her, and she rose and began to serve Him. (Matthew 8:14-17)

An incredible reality surrounds the beginning of the ministry of the Apostle Peter, as Jesus heals someone very dear to him. We know little about Peter's family background, but we do know one of the first things Peter experienced when answering the call to follow Jesus was the healing of his mother-in-law. When I consider Peter, the 'in your face', 'rough and tumble', 'speak first, think later' kind of guy that he was, I'm confident his assurance rose out of what he witnessed in the beginning of his ministry. Miracles give us confidence. Peter was confident, sometimes even a bit over the top. Immediately following the healing, Peter's mother-in-law rose to serve the One who just brought her healing. I suspect, like Peter, she, too, spent a lifetime in service to the Serving King.

As we watch the life of Peter, we see the Lord healing and doing various miracles that Peter was directly or indirectly involved with. I think this is why we see Peter writing later in his own epistle... "cast all your cares on Him for He cares for you" (I Peter 5:7). I believe his profound confidence, trust, and assurance began in Peter's mind with the healing of his mother-in-law. Because of this firsthand experience, Jesus was able to help instill confidence in Peter, a confidence he would need in the days to follow.

Do you find yourself as a 'Peter' at times, overly confident because of what you have seen Jesus do in the lives of those you love most? Are you sometimes 'king of not thinking through' the consequences of your confidence? Or do you wonder at times if you are not worthy, or that maybe others have done too much wrong to be made right by Jesus? If you ever think those thoughts, reflect on the 'think before you speak' disciple named Peter and know that God, too, can and will work through you. Knowing you are loved by the Serving King will give you the confidence to love on...

TM

The Contagious Nature Of Healing

"Nothing is so healing as the human touch." —Bobby Fischer

That evening they brought to Him many who were oppressed by demons, and He cast out the spirits with a word and healed all who were sick. This was to fulfill what was spoken by the prophet Isaiah: "He took our illnesses and bore our diseases.   (Matthew 8:14-17)

In this passage, we see Jesus performing a miracle in the very beginning stages of His ministry. And Peter, a novice to chasing after the Serving King, soon realizes this is just the beginning. Jesus was invited to Peter's house shortly after Peter made his commitment to follow Him. He accepted the invitation to become a fisher of men. Little did he know how soon the wounded and broken would find their way to Jesus.

Miracles, especially miracles of healing, soon draw a crowd. People began bringing the wounded and broken, the physically sick, even those demonically oppressed. And with every healing, the power of God's Word, whether they understood it or not, began to unfold, "He took our illnesses and bore our diseases" (Isaiah53:4).

We find in Scripture that Jesus at regular times would 'speak' to sickness, disease, and infirmities, commanding 'them' to come out and/ or loose the person. In Luke 13, Jesus saw a woman crippled with a spirit of infirmity and He spoke to her, laying hands on her, and she was healed. In the book of Matthew chapter 8, we see Jesus healing many more people, 'speaking' to the disease, even the weather obeyed His commands.

Healing is contagious, spreading rapidly across the land. And nothing has changed. People still long for the healing touch of the Master's hand. Understand, He has invited you to touch the lives of others. His touch is now at your fingertips. Healing begins with the human touch. Love on in the way of the Serving King…
TM

DAY 82

Where are we home?

"I'm no leader; I'm a little humble follower." —Mohammed Ali

Now when Jesus saw a crowd around Him, He gave orders to go over to the other side. And a scribe came up and said to Him, "Teacher, I will follow You wherever You go." And Jesus said to him, "Foxes have holes, and birds of the air have nests, but the Son of Man has nowhere to lay His head."

(Matthew 8:18-20)

There is comfort found in laying one's head on the familiar pillow of home. It offers a sense of the known, a safe place. Here, we find a man who is associated with a group that typically stands against Christ. Theirs is the life of comfort, the life of a scribe. But now, this man wants to be a disciple, following this Rabbi who does miracles and gathers crowds. To follow Christ is to allow a transformation to start and continue in your life; it is not only a spectacle to witness. This man might not even realize what he is asking for.

Christ does not welcome nor turn him away, He simply admits the reality of being a follower. It is not the life that the scribe knows. It is not filled with food for every meal, encouragement from the larger society, and there is not even a place to lay one's head. The creatures of the earth have this simple luxury, but to be a disciple means that you no longer have it. To be a disciple, your life needs to go through a transformation. It means you are guided by the Spirit and lay your head down where possible and where guided. To truly be a follower means that there is a perfecting of your life and actions, as the Spirit works through your whole being.

This is a freeing life. By not having a bed, you are mobile. You are free to roam where led. It means you can find comfort in the unknown and unfamiliar. Why can you do this? Could it be because you understand that the most familiar thing is not constricted to a place either? The Spirit of God is no longer tied to a single place or person but free among the children of God and among all nations. The Spirit is no longer only found in the temple; it is out among the people. It is found in and through the people. The Spirit is where our home is found. Keep loving…
KD

His Voice

*"The other disciples told Thomas that they had seen Jesus, but Thomas doubted—
'Except I shall see ..., I will not believe.' Thomas needed the personal touch of
Jesus. When His touches come, or how they come, we do not know; but when they
do come they are indescribably precious. 'My Lord and my God!'"*
—*Oswald Chambers*

**"And Jesus said to him, "Follow Me, and leave the dead to bury their own
dead."** (Matthew 8:22)

Many are those who begin the quest at the encouragement of other
trekkers, trusted peers whose opinions matter; but for those who journey
deep into the trek after the Serving King, the encouragement of trusted
others can never sustain. The trek is simply too difficult to endure
under the tutorage and encouragement of anyone but the Serving King.
Learning to hear His voice, amidst the voices of competing 'trusted
peers', can be tricksy for those plodding along immersed in the fraternity
of trusted peers.

Therein lies the problem for the many who dream of joining those
trusted peers deep into the being of Jesus, as the mob pushes them along,
deeper and deeper into crushing challenges that lay ahead. These trusted
peers, loyal as they may be, cannot sustain you as the degree of difficulty
in following Him continues to increase; especially, when His demands
seem so outrageous. Nor will Jesus allow those who hear His voice to
remain behind, caring for the novices, those well-intentioned trekkers,
who follow the 'flock', doing what sheep do, yet never hearing the
Shepherd call them by name.

Eventually, every trekker has their moment of shock, disbelief at
what Jesus is suggesting. It is unavoidable for those who trek deep
into the quest after Jesus. The trek is simply too overwhelming. So,
you must pause now and again, break free from the 'flock' which is
not yet your own, and listen carefully. Have you heard Him call you
by name, or are you simply caught in the 'flock', heeding the call of
well-intentioned trekkers who have heard their name whispered by the
Shepherd, assuming you have heard the Shepherd call yours as well?
You dare not simply get caught up in the movement of the flock, unless
you also hear His voice, for He leads them to places only the 'called-out
ones' dare to traverse in the days yet ahead. Listen and love on in the
way of the Serving King...
DM

DAY 84

Shall We Wake Him?

"There are stages in life when there is no storm... it is when a crisis arises that we instantly reveal upon whom we rely. If we have been learning to worship God and to trust Him, the crisis will reveal that we will go to the breaking point and not break in our confidence in Him." —Oswald Chambers

And He said to them, "Why are you afraid, O you of little faith?" Then He rose and rebuked the winds and the sea, and there was a great calm. (Matthew 8:26)

Calm seas are delightful in life's journey as you trek after the Serving King. But they never ever last, even for the most faithful trekkers. It simply is not the way of God. His ways are not our ways. Rough seas and winds are often part of the quest.

Yet, it is the proximity of the Serving King that baffles the child sailing along the seas of life. The storms are expected in moments when you have drifted, or outright abandoned the trek, leaving Jesus on the shore while you sail on alone. Too often, we bask in a false bravado that comes with months and years of smooth sailing in the infancy stage of your journey; and yes, all of life, in some sense, is the mere 'infancy of the journey' with the Christ. But this raging storm arose while you kept Him close, even in the boat, 'sailing' along in precisely the manner He has instructed. Still, the storm rages as the Serving King slumbers just steps away. Can this really be? A storm when Jesus is so close, when your being and doing has never been finer?

His sleeping will bother you, perhaps, even anger you, thinking His sleeping renders Him unaware of the 'raging storm' consuming you. But He is never 'unawares'. This storm, too, has purpose; like every calm sea, they are but 'flip sides' of the same coin in your trek after the 'sleeping King'. His slumbering, intentional in every way, is the pathway to "... the crisis revealing that we will go to the breaking point and not break our confidence in Him." There it is, the breaking point, tempting you to wake Him from His peaceful slumber. Then those crushing words, "O you of little faith." And the calm seas return, but they are not the blessing of God; no, the blessing was the raging storm, and you have surrendered that blessing for the moment. But for now, calm seas it must be. But fear not, one day you too shall sail with vigor in the blessing of 'raging seas', while the King slumbers in your boat, 'loving' you all the while...
DM

The Tough Places

"Look back at your own experience, and you will find that until you learned Who Jesus was, you were a cunning sceptic about His power. When you were on the mount, you could believe anything, but what about the time when you were up against facts in the valley?" —Oswald Chambers

"...And when He came to the other side, to the country of the Gadarenes, two demon possessed men met Him, coming out of the tombs, so fierce that no one could pass." (Matthew 8:28)

It is the "tough places", not just any tough place, but your tough place, that threatens to erode your 'mountaintop' confidence in the Serving King. The 'blessed assurance' of the mountain often quickly erodes in the 'tough place', that dangerous place where "...so fierce no one could pass that way," unfolds in its rough and tumble manner. And sooner or later, the trek after the Serving King takes you to that tough place. It is here, face to face with the 'no one could pass that way', that the optimism of the mountaintop must show its mettle in the 'fire' of reality, a reality that is far beyond what you can solve. There are some things that only the Serving King can address. The quicker you learn this reality, the better.

You will be tempted to retreat to the mountaintop, leaving the tough places and those pleading for your assistance, to fend for themselves. But you can know no such retreat. Instead, pleading for compassion, they will press you over and over again, "But if you can do anything..." And, indeed, you will attempt many 'anythings', but, alas, you are never the solution. In the end, all you can do is point to the One who can. And the many will demand so much more than a pathway to the One who can really do what only the Serving King can do.

Thus, in the end, it is never about what you can do; instead, it is always about what the Serving King can do in your stead. Your task is to simply point them to the mountaintop, the place where Jesus reveals who He really is, what He can do for those who believe. "All things are possible for those who believe" (Mark 9:23). And therein lies the key to 'proving your mettle'. Can you believe in the face of the tough places? Dare you boldly march into the place, "...so fierce no one could pass that way." Love dares to pass that way...
DM

The Cost Of Loving

"Natural devotion may be all very well to attract us to Jesus, to make us feel His fascination, but it will never make us disciples. Natural devotion will always deny Jesus somewhere or other." —Oswald Chambers

So, they came out and went into the pigs, and behold, the whole herd rushed down the steep back and into the sea and drowned in the waters. The herdsmen fled... (Matthew 8:32-33)

'Loving as Jesus loved' is quite simply the essence of the Christian experience, and it is inevitably costly, more costly than anyone could anticipate. Pigs, seemingly mundane to us, were the essence of this community now on the verge of bankruptcy and hunger. Little wonder, the herdsmen fled, informing everyone of just how expensive this Jesus was going to be for this little community. Thus, the cost of following Jesus was suddenly more relevant and immediate than anyone could have imagined. Jesus or not, Son of God or not, this Jesus had to go.

The transition from 'recipient' of love to 'giver' of love is tantamount to 'losing one's life' for the sake of others. The 'others', men tormented by the demonic, were no longer distant neighbors, inexpensive and out of mind. No, these men were suddenly costly in the worst possible way in the here and now. Hence, you will be tempted to say with the crowd, "Lord, please leave." And He will, simply because you have asked. It is His way.

So, for now, simply "...love one another," your brothers and sisters, those who will love you back, those who are inexpensive and easy. And yes, even that will be much harder than you have imagined.

But understand, a time will come, perhaps, a time much sooner than you expect, when the cost of following Jesus will present itself again. The Serving King often returns at the most inopportune times, asking for more than we have dared to consider, even our pigs. Until that moment, rest in the comfort of your family, learn the basics of love. There will be plenty of time to learn the cost of love farther down the road...
DM

Costly

"Jesus says, in effect, 'Do not be bothered with whether you are being justly dealt with or not.' To look for justice is a sign of deflection from devotion to Him. Never look for justice in this world, but never cease to give it. If we look for justice, we will begin to grouse and to indulge in the discontent of self-pity—'Why should I be treated like this?' If we are devoted to Jesus Christ we have nothing to do with what we meet, whether it is just or unjust." —Oswald Chambers

And behold, all the city came out to meet Jesus, and when they say Him, they begged Him to leave their region. (Matthew 8:34)

Deep into the trek after the Serving King, an alarm will quietly begin to rage deep within your being, as you begin to notice an increasing lack of 'justice' in the world around you. While a lack of justice in the life of another will disturb you greatly at times, the quiet, raging alarm will not disable your trek after the Serving King, until that tragic moment, for life is a tragedy, when 'justice' eludes you. It is in the moment of 'lost personal justice' that the trek may come to a sudden halt, for few of us are well-suited to a life without 'personal justice'. Few are prepared for the cost of pigs.

Understand, it is not the total absence of justice in your life, rather, those glaring moments when justice eludes your pursuit, ushering in a hesitancy to continue the trek. You will be tempted to return to childhood rants, "That's not fair," and refuse to move forward in your trek. And He will respond to you from His station on the cross, "No, it is not." In that moment, His challenge to disregard personal justice rings forth, "... deny yourself, take up your cross and follow Me" (Mark 8:34). It is this moment of 'Gospel clarity' that devotion to the ways of God becomes crystal clear, creating a new reality for those who trek after the Serving King, a reality in which grace trumps justice as Christ-followers 'take up their cross' and abandon claims for personal justice to reign.

Clearly, this is not a trek for the many, but for the few who '...take up His cross'. This is not a call to be a Simon of Cyrene (Matthew 27:32) carrying His cross; to the contrary, it is the call to leave personal justice behind and take up your cross'. 'Take up his cross' is the quintessence of devotion to Christ. But be warned, justice will not go 'quietly into the night'; rather, the silent alarm will, more often than not, rage on deep within you. Dare to love on in the ways of the Serving King...
DM

Faith in Action!

"Do you want to know who you are? Don't ask. Act! Action will delineate and define you." —Thomas Jefferson

And getting into a boat He crossed over and came to His own city. And behold, some people brought to Him a paralytic, lying on a bed. And when Jesus saw their faith, He said to the paralytic, "Take heart, My son; your sins are forgiven." (Matthew 9:1-2)

How many times have you heard, "Be the hands and feet of Christ?" This saying became a reality when I memorized my first verse, 1 John 3:18, as a young seminarian nearly 20 years ago. This Scripture states: "Little children, let us not love in word or talk but in deed and in truth." I understood the saying meant that as a Christian I am called to put my faith into action.

In other words, Christianity is not a spectator sport. One doesn't become mature in the faith by watching others and cheering them on. One becomes mature by pressing forward toward the goal. In today's reading from Matthew, Jesus demonstrates this Scripture to perfection. Jesus witnesses not only the physical act of carrying a paralyzed man, He sees deeper into their hearts. He sees their faith—in action.

But you might be thinking that faith is believing in "things not seen" (Heb. 11:1). Jesus could certainly see the helpers carrying the man, right? But Jesus had a spiritual radar which we, if not honed through prayer, seldom utilize. We might have seen the paralytic's helpers and thought, "Why are they helping this paralyzed man? Are they colleagues and they saw the man fall off a roof working to feed his family? Was the man born that way and these helpers saw Jesus heal several people in the past thinking now He could heal their friend?" Jesus looked past their obvious laborious effort to carry the man. Jesus saw men stepping up to the plate with the hearts to serve this paralyzed man.

Today, be the hands and feet of Christ. Step up to the plate and get involved in the game of life. Serve the person in your circle of influence who may be paralyzed emotionally, mentally, physically, or spiritually! Actualize loving like the Serving King...

JP

Cutting to the Cancerous Heart!

"Knowing that you are completely forgiven destroys the power of sin in your life."
— Joseph Prince

And behold, some of the scribes said to themselves, "This man is blaspheming." But Jesus, knowing their thoughts, said, "Why do you think evil in your hearts? For which is easier, to say, 'Your sins are forgiven,' or to say, 'Rise and walk'? But that you may know that the Son of Man has authority on earth to forgive sins"—He then said to the paralytic—"Rise, pick up your bed and go home."
(Matthew 9:1-8)

Yesterday, I challenged you to put your faith into action. Today, let's focus on Jesus' action or lack thereof. He did the opposite of what the carnal men thought Jesus should do. Rather than telling the paralyzed man to get up, pick up his mat, and walk, which would have been easier in man's eyes and far more braggadocios, the Serving King presses into the deeper issues of life.

Stop right there; hit the pause button, or as my grandmother would have said, "Hold your horses!" He said what? Imagine yourself in this scene. You see a paralyzed man being carried. You probably have witnessed Jesus healing others of leprosy, blindness, and lameness. You don't know Jesus eventually tells the man to stand and walk. All you hear Him say is the man's sins are forgiven. How could He say this and seemingly do nothing? While the scribes, and I dare say many other bystanders, were looking at the outward appearance of the paralyzed man, Jesus knew in His heart the man was a sinner in need of something far greater than a physical healing. He also knew what the scribes were thinking!

As a chaplain at a cancer hospital, I have a philosophy of care—If we heal every patient every time through modern medicine, but do nothing to treat the heart, we have failed the patient and committed what I call, "medical or spiritual malpractice." A broken heart is harder to diagnose as needing medical or spiritual care, but it, nonetheless, needs attention. Jesus saw through the obvious physical paralysis and cut right to the cancerous hearts of both the paralyzed man and, I hope, the scribes. His words penetrated to the marrow of their hearts and truly healed him, setting him free, and, hopefully, setting the scribes free as well. I challenge you to look into a man's heart, offer forgiveness, and set that man free! Let everyone experience the love of the Serving King...
JP

DAY 90

The Gift of Authority!

"The wisest have the most authority." —Plato

When the crowds saw it, they were afraid, and they glorified God, who had given such authority to men.   (Matthew 9:8)

What did the crowds see? What was 'it'? They saw the man, once paralyzed, now walking; he got up and went to his home. What a miracle! Jesus healed the paralyzed man; case closed, end of the story. Yet, they still missed the point. They missed 'it'.

Jesus gave a glimpse into the Kingdom of God, "But that you may know that the Son of Man has authority on earth to forgive sins." He then said to the paralytic, "Rise, pick up your bed, and go home." The point: Jesus has the authority to tell the man to get up, and He has the authority to grant forgiveness. How did they miss this point?

What is perplexing to me is the latter part of the aforementioned Scripture; "...they were afraid, and they glorified God, who had given such authority to men." What does 'men' mean? What authority has He given to humanity (anthrōpos)? The greatest mistake by the crowd was that they thought Jesus was still a human being; they still saw Him as the Son of Man from the line of David and not the Son of God. His authority is inherently His. He is the Son of God.

Most of society looks in the wrong place for authority. We look at degrees, or superiors, or titles, all seeming to grant authority. But our authority comes from Jesus, by way of the cross, giving us all the authority we need.

The people were not silent or stunned at the miracle. No, they "glorified God"! They praised God for His miraculous healing, and rightfully so. But, what did they do with the authority 'given to men'? It appears they were not ready to see Jesus as the Christ. They only saw Jesus the carpenter. Praise Jesus, the carpenter, but take the authority from Jesus the Christ as your gift to cast evil away in His Name. Utilize the love of the Serving King...

JP

Follow Me

"The best leaders are following Christ. That's the best leader you can follow."
—*Tony Dungy*

As Jesus went on from there, He saw a man named Matthew sitting at the tax collector's booth. "Follow Me," He told him, and Matthew got up and followed Him. (Matthew 9:9)

Matthew followed Jesus, presumably without hesitation, as did the other disciples. He would have known that Jesus' invitation was not a temporary reprieve from his work. The word 'follow' here means to accept and follow leadership, command, or guidance. Matthew would certainly have heard of Jesus as He just finished a tour of miracles and deliverances from Gadarenes to Capernaum.

We know tax collectors were quite often deceptive and charged more than necessary in order to line their own pockets. This may or may not have been Matthew's practice, but, either way, he had a solid, good paying job. Why would he leave it to follow and become a disciple of One who does not have a place to lay His head?

Perhaps, Matthew had been listening to the better way Jesus had to offer. He was tired of the rat race and deception he was carrying on day after day. Maybe he determined money was not as satisfying as he had heard. Recall here that Jesus knows every man's thoughts (John 2:25). Jesus knew Matthew's heart was ready to receive His leadership, and he would ditch the life offered by the world and follow Him.

Even more important than the initial call of any disciple is the ongoing call to follow Jesus as the leader of your life. As Matthew knew, this was a radical career change. And we must know when we get up to follow Jesus, it is a lifetime commitment. We must make the decision every day that we will follow Him. Regardless of our profession or lack thereof, we have to make a cognizant decision that no matter what comes our way, we will follow. Have you made that decision today? Are you making it every day? Saying yes to Jesus is not a one-time gig. It was never intended to be a temporary break from reality; rather, a life-changing event that would begin the development of the new creation fully engaged in loving like the Serving King...
MR

DAY 92

A Feast for Sinners

"The best leaders are following Christ. That's the best leader you can follow."
—Mick Mars

…many tax collectors and sinners came and ate with Him and His disciples. When the Pharisees saw this, they asked His disciples, "Why does your Teacher eat with tax collectors and sinners?" On hearing this, Jesus said, "It is not the healthy who need a doctor, but the sick. But go and learn what this means: 'I desire mercy, not sacrifice.' For I have not come to call the righteous, but sinners." (Matthew 9:10-13)

Jesus proved when He began calling His disciples that He was not living according to the status quo. First of all, it was not typical that a teacher would call his disciples. Usually, they would be clamoring for his attention and hoping they would be accepted. Secondly, specifically with His selection of Matthew, He demonstrated that He calls people to follow Him even while they are sinners! This completely rocked the paradigm of the Pharisees. A teacher of the law would not have even been in the company of such a disgraced person, let alone call them to sit at their feet and learn their ways.

And then, there is the casual and unexpected environment of a dinner at Matthew's house. We don't know how much time had passed between Matthew's call before he invited his friends to meet Jesus, but I presume it was not much. I love Matthew's enthusiasm as he invites his friends to meet the One who has extended mercy and grace to him. Isn't that what you would do? Isn't that what you have done? Or have you? Have you held a dinner or some other event that allowed your not-yet-believing friends an opportunity to meet Jesus? Have you gathered the ones you care about to make sure they have the same opportunity for grace?

Maybe, initially you did, but if you are like most mature disciples in the western world, those invitations have long faded and expired. You are walking and spending time with other disciples now. It may be that your whole circle of friends has changed. Sometimes that is necessary to help you move out of sin. But there should still be opportunities to hold an event like Matthew's, meant for other sinners to be introduced to Jesus. Be careful you don't fall into the trap of the Pharisees and begin thinking your personal sacrifice for King Jesus is more important than intentionally extending mercy to others. Loving like the Serving King begins with mercy…

MR

The Reception

"The highest reward for a person's toil is not what they get for it, but what they become by it." —John Ruskin

Then the disciples of John came to Him, saying, "Why do we and the Pharisees fast, but Your disciples do not fast?" And Jesus said to them, "Can the wedding guests mourn as long as the bridegroom is with them? The days will come when the bridegroom is taken away from them, and then they will fast.

(Matthew 9:14-15)

Not long ago, while officiating a funeral, I found myself audience to a chorus I'd heard many, many times before. For the sake of copyright, I'll withhold the actual lyrics, but I'll give you a quick compositional synopsis: This life is pain, toil, and drudgery, but someday I'll sprout wings and fly to be with Jesus. I wrestled with those words.

It is undeniable that life has its share of pain. Live for long, and you'll understand there is brokenness and hurt in every corner of existence, no one is exempt. Here in this passage of Matthew, we find the disciples of John in a period of fasting, waiting, and anticipating the One who, in the words of the prophet Isaiah, would come, "…to bind up the brokenhearted, to proclaim freedom for the captives, and release from darkness for the prisoners." Jesus makes no mistake in classifying the intent of their fasting as mourning. The people of God were captive: in the political sense to the Roman authorities, but, more importantly, to the sin and corruption that had initially led them there. Jesus makes it very clear to them here; the wait is over. The bridegroom has come. This is no longer a funeral; it's a wedding, and the groom has come to redeem His bride.

Forgiveness is the beginning of a life full of hope and purpose. Yes, the troubles still come, and there is pain to be endured, but do we truly understand that even now the Spirit of the Living God is with us? We don't have to wait for Heaven to see the joy of the Lord manifest powerfully in our midst. Praise God! As the church, we undergo intentional seasons of celebration, anticipation, and fasting. Each have their place but are undergirded in the truth that Christ has already come to release us from both the penalty and power of sin. So, let us live lives that reflect His joy right here and right now, instead of waiting to do it someday when this life is over. Express the love of the Serving King…

DR

DAY 94

You Are More

"For me, forgiveness and compassion are always linked: how do we hold people accountable for wrongdoing and yet at the same time remain in touch with their humanity enough to believe in their capacity to be transformed?" —Bell Hooks

"No one puts a piece of unshrunk cloth on an old garment, for the patch tears away from the garment, and a worse tear is made. Neither is new wine put into old wineskins. If it is, the skins burst and the wine is spilled and the skins are destroyed. But new wine is put into fresh wineskins, and so both are preserved."

(Matthew 9:16-17)

Everywhere Jesus tread, old things were made brand new. Just prior to these two verses, a paralyzed man was forgiven by Christ. But demonstrating the truly life-changing power of those words, that same man rose to his feet and quite literally carried his deathbed home with him. Matthew, a tax collector, was considered a scoundrel and a thief among his fellow Jews – the scum of the earth. Jesus came with the call to follow, and Matthew was no longer a man of ill repute, but a disciple under the tutelage of a Rabbi with authority none had seen before.

Forgiveness is essential to the life of those in Christ, and, thankfully, we have a God that stopped short of nothing, giving His own Son as final payment for our sin. Forgiveness is ours forever because of this! Yet, what we so often overlook is that which proceeds from forgiveness is a life that is forever altered by this new reality. We're not just given a new station; we're a new creation (2 Cor. 5:17).

"I'm just a sinner saved by grace," goes the old adage I've heard in Christian circles for years. No! Reject that notion! By the transforming grace of God, you're not just a sinner. You were a sinner, and now you're a new creation that is holy and pleasing in God's sight and ready to be filled and used for His glory. Do not settle for less, and do not let the enemy convince you that mercy is the only grace you receive. Victory and renewal are just as much a part of His plan. He reminds us today, through the symbols of patches and wineskins, that because of Him, we can be renewed in such a way that the Holy Spirit can fill us, rather than destroy us. We can be intricately woven back into His plan for our lives without being an ill fit in the Kingdom. He's done the work of restoring us. Now, let's love like the Serving King...

DR

The Touch That Transforms...

"A Christian worker has to learn how to be God's noble man or woman amid a crowd of ignoble things." —Oswald Chambers

And behold, a woman who had suffered from a discharge of blood for twelve years came up behind Him and touched the fringe of His Garment, for she said to herself, "If only I touch the fringe of His garment I will be made well..."

(Matthew 9:21)

It is a strange dichotomy for those deep into the trek after the Serving King, realizing the more 'noble' the Christian worker becomes, the more 'ignoble' surroundings become. Understand, the condition of the 'crowd of ignoble things', once a cozy atmosphere for you, has not changed at all, even slightly. The change, 'regeneration' of the highest kind, the fruit of 'born again', occurs in the Christian worker, forever making 'ignoble' those things yet untouched by the transformative power of the Holy Spirit.

And you will be tempted to think, "I can no longer lounge in the crowd of the ignoble," and for a season, very early in the trek, that will indeed be the case. But the Serving King has not produced 'nobility' in you to remove you from the 'ignoble' of this world; rather, the 'noble' taking shape in you is precisely to enable you to 'dwell' in the land crowded with 'ignoble things'. But it will not be comfortable for those deep into the trek.

And yes, it is this very dichotomy that ushers in the sense of 'alienness', haunting every child trekking after the Serving King, "...my Kingdom is not of this world" (John 18:36). And great is the temptation to leave the 'crowd of ignoble things'. Refusing to 'become weak, that I might win the weak', too leery of tarnishing the 'noble' finally taking shape in you. You are fearful you may run back to the 'ignoble' long before the 'noble' has taken shape, damaging the yet fragile 'noble' taking shape deep within the depths of your being.

The great challenge for the Christian worker is to "...learn how to be God's noble man or woman amid a crowd of ignoble things." Only then can you 'become weak' to win the weak. This is a challenge far too great to engage in alone. It is the zenith of the trek after the Serving King, only available to those who have undergone the most profound layers of regeneration, enabling the noble saint to "...became weak, that I might win the weak." Take the hand of Jesus and the hand of a 'noble saint', and dare to trek where only the few can ever go. Love demands you walk with Him amongst the wounded and bleeding...

DM

DAY 96

Your Faith Has Made You Well

"When I stand face to face with Jesus Christ and He says to me—"Believest thou this?" I find that faith is as natural as breathing, and I am staggered that I was so stupid as not to trust Him before." —Oswald Chambers

Jesus turned, and seeing her He said, "Take heart, daughter; your faith has made you well." And instantly the woman was made well. (Matthew 9:22)

The crisis of opportunity, crashing into this present moment, with a demand for immediate affirmation, generates an awkward moment for the child trekking after the Serving King. And that awkwardness is amplified greatly by the degree of difficulty concerning the opportunity now available. You will pause and ask, "Is this reasonable?" No, it is not in a world yet untouched by the arrival of the Kingdom of God. The woman, not yet understanding the immediate arrival of the Kingdom of God, dares to dream of a future yet to come. Her mind cannot grasp the arrival of the Kingdom of God in this very moment, healing in the here and now. This is simply unreasonable, beyond what the rational mind can grasp.

Therein lies the 'awkward moment', interwoven with the arrival of the Kingdom of God with its entirely new way of being; a 'newness' hampered only by a willingness to release faith in all of its Spirit-induced power. A 'faith' ushering in a reality reflecting the Kingdom of God, far exceeding what we have been able to 'see' thus far, "Now to Him who is able to do far more abundantly than all that we ask or think, according to the power at work within us" (Ephesians 3:20). A new way of being has arrived. Your world can never be the same. You cannot go back. The awkward moment has arrived, new ways of seeing, impossible in days gone by.

You will resist its call, pushing you toward ways of being and doing, new ways of seeing and thinking, new ways of exercising faith in a world now encompassed by the Kingdom of God, the power of God. Nonetheless, there He is, He has found you, exposing you to the ways of the Kingdom of God. And then the awkward moment as the light of revelation pours into your vision, "Dare I touch the fringe of His garment?" This trek has come to a turning point. You can travel no farther until you do. Go ahead, dare to touch the fringe of His garment as He passes by. His love awaits…

DM

Mercy

"When we discern that people are not going on spiritually and allow the discernment to turn to criticism, we block our way to God. God never gives us discernment in order that we may criticize, but that we may intercede."
—*Oswald Chambers*

Two blind men followed Him, crying aloud, "Have mercy on us Son of David… And Jesus said to them, "Do you believe that I am able to do this?"
(Matthew 9:27-28)

Spiritual discernment, the ability to understand the spiritual condition of another, typically comes very late in the trek after the Serving King. It is a mammoth responsibility. And with it comes a great temptation to respond poorly, to use discernment as a sword of judgment, rather than a vehicle of grace and intercession. And the temptation to judge increases proportionally in relationship to expectations, creating the conditions of a perfect storm, a radical abandonment of your purpose in discernment. Misunderstanding the purpose of discernment, grace, and intercession, you will be tempted to take on the role of Him who "…will convict the world concerning sin" (John 16:8), mimicking His voice, attempting to set straight those whose lives "…are not going on spiritually." But discernment is not meant to be a sword of conviction in your hands. That is the role of He who comes.

Spiritual discernment in the hands of those trekking after the Serving King has a very different purpose, equally redemptive as the work of conviction by the Holy Spirit, ultimately unleashing the power of God in those who seemingly are stuck, "…not going on spiritually." Yours are the hands catching those whom the Spirit has convicted. No person is well equipped to endure the conviction of the Holy Spirit. His conviction overpowers, cutting to the core, crippling those upon whom conviction falls. And so, the one gifted with discernment becomes 'The Catcher', warned by the Holy Spirit to be ready, for the Spirit is about to work in ways only He can, rendering those so convicted, stumbling, falling.

Resist the temptation to be more than 'The Catcher'; instead, chastising the fallen, with yet another blistering conviction, unleashed by the chosen One, called out by the Spirit to 'catch'. Simply catch those who are reeling. You knew the fall was coming, the fruit of discernment well within your sight. And yes, 'catching the convicted' is often difficult, their reactions varied, different in so many ways. But the Spirit chose you to be 'The Catcher' because you can. Love on in the way of the Serving King…
DM

Now That You Can See

"All God's revelations are sealed until they are opened to us by obedience. You will never get them open by philosophy or thinking. Immediately you obey, a flash of light comes". —Oswald Chambers

Then He touched their eyes, saying, "According to your faith be it done for you." And their eyes were opened. (Matthew 9:29-30)

We would like to think revelation comes in sweeping, comprehensive packages, allowing the child trekking after the Serving King to gradually embrace this or that dimension, implementing revelation in what is deemed to be appropriately manageable pieces, but such is not the case. Revelation comes in complete packages, invested with meaning and purpose for the present moment and consequent moments to follow. And therein lies the secret to 'revelatory moments' of all kinds, unleashing truth and meaning in the immediacy of the present moment.

And the 'childlikeness' does not point to an intellectual simplicity as the many novices would like you to believe, proposing a shallow and overly simplistic approach to life and faith; instead, to the childlike obedience of those who seize revelatory tidbits and quickly go about the tricksy business of applying the revelation they have received in and for the present moment. The 'child' is not childlike in simplicity of thought and faith; rather, the simplicity of immediate 'childlike' obedience.

The 'hidden things' are not overly simplistic, rendering 'mind' moot and unnecessary; instead, the hidden things are the 'points of application' for the immediate context of immensely complicated being and doing in the life of faith. And yes, it is the application of the hidden things enabling one to be childlike, obedience to what is revealed, applied to the specific particulars of individual lives. And so, the cry for childlike simplicity of thought, often the battle cry of the novice, or the lazy, unwilling to engage in the hard work of 'thinking' deeply, is rendered irrelevant to the life of faith sought by those who trek deep into the being and doing of Jesus. And yes, learning the 'how to' of applied faith is extremely complicated, often 'hidden', only made known by the Spirit of God to those who are radically childlike, obedient in the immediate context. Dare to see and the love in the way of the Serving King…
DM

DAY 99

Come And See

"A good commander is benevolent and unconcerned with fame." —*Sun Tzu*

And Jesus sternly warned them, "See that no one knows about it." But they went and spread His fame through all that district. (Matthew 9:30-31)

The early optimism, infused with vitality as the 'easy' transformations unfold, layers of 'sin residue' quickly giving way, giving birth to a 'showroom' mentality, "...come and see what God has done in me!" But soon, the showroom luster fades, as the Serving King, unconcerned with external appearances, begins the messy process of rooting out the 'inner stains' of original sin, seemingly unconcerned with who sees your messy state while parading you, bound in 'absolute captivity' around the neighborhood, yes, your neighborhood. It is only then, in your conquered state, realizing the Serving King is not nearly so concerned with 'appearance' as you are paraded. It dawns on you what this 'parade' is all about.

It has not been, and never will be, ultimately about with your 'showroom' worthiness. That is religion, and the Serving King has little or no interest; instead, His interest in 'parading you' is entirely about exhibiting 'absolute captivity' as the conquered soul is remodeled in the most profound manner possible. The confusion, of course, arises out of the showroom worthiness of those who are being transformed by the power and presence of the Holy Spirit. But be warned, the intention of the Serving King is to provide so much more than an external 'buff and wax'.

You will struggle as the showroom readiness disappears as He mines deeper and deeper into your being and doing, dust and debris clouding the air. And you will beg and plead with Him not to expose you as He whittles away at the sin stained being and doing that has been you for these many years. But whining will do no good. The Serving King knows only authenticity; it is the only way He knows to conquer, and conquered you are. But those watching the parade, ugly as it may be at times, see your changing countenance, the warm and pleasant smile, the utter joy that is yours as the Serving King parades you. And yes, the 'fragrance of Him everywhere' fills the air. And the many begin to yearn to be in that conquered parade. Love on in the way of the Serving King...
DM

Us Verses Them

"Faith activates God - Fear activates the Enemy." —Joel Osteen

As they were going away, behold, a demon-oppressed man who was mute was brought to Him. And when the demon had been cast out, the mute man spoke. And the crowds marveled, saying, "Never was anything like this seen in Israel." But the Pharisees said, "He casts out demons by the prince of demons."

(Matthew 9:32-34)

I remember growing up and playing a variety of sports. One part of sports that has always fascinated me is the fostering of an 'us versus them' mindset. We could not be friends with anyone from another team, nor could we help them when they were struggling in our battle. They were the enemy, always the enemy, and it seemed like no matter what woes came, the easy solution was to blame it on 'them'. Our task was to overcome 'them' at any cost. And, most importantly, if you were not one of us, you were one of them.

As a culture, we have done the same thing in most aspects of our lives. Life has become one big 'us against them'. It seems that anytime something happens that we are uncomfortable with, we want to have someone to blame it on, a 'them' who has created the problem.

This event in the Gospel shows that same mindset. Jesus healed people, those who were mute could speak, those who were blind could see, even the lame could walk! People, especially people of faith, should have rejoiced in His great work. Instead, they chose to say that He could only do it, because He worked for the devil. Really? Unfortunately, we often share this idea in the church today. Anytime someone does something for the Lord that makes us uncomfortable or is too different, we often attack them and make them the enemy.

My prayer and challenge for us all today is that we could rejoice when God restores people! That we could focus on the hope He brings for redemption and not try to create more enemies. What is God doing in your life? Who is He using? Is the end result more important than the messenger? God heals people daily, and we need to embrace the work and rejoice with those He touches. Love on in the way of the Serving King…

SV

Lost and Found

"The purpose of human life is to serve, and to show compassion and the will to help others." —Albert Schweitzer

And Jesus went throughout all the cities and villages, teaching in their synagogues and proclaiming the Gospel of the kingdom and healing every disease and every affliction. When He saw the crowds, He had compassion for them, because they were harassed and helpless, like sheep without a shepherd.

(Matthew 9:35-36)

The Serving King traveled, going to many of the synagogues to share the truth of the Gospel. He also continued His ministry of healing, bringing hope and healing to those who needed it most. I am reminded by this tale of just how often the Serving King comes looking for His lost children.

I remember one instance as a child when I became separated from my family in Costco. And rest assured, I knew I was lost. There was no doubt in my young mind. The fear and desperation falling on me was overwhelming. In that moment, all I wanted was someone who loved me to come and rescue me. Tragically, many of those who are lost have yet to discover their lostness. It is the great tragedy of life.

I think Jesus sees most people like a lost child, desperately needing to be rescued. Sadly, they often are unaware of just how lost they really are. Still, Jesus was moved with compassion, because He saw people wandering through life like sheep lost with no shepherd to help them. Sheep, like me, have an easy time getting lost, and cannot find our way back without a shepherd. God sees us as lost sheep and wants to be the loving figure that brings us home.

I am becoming more and more like Jesus as I chase after Him. I beginning to feel compassion for those who are lost and have yet to realize it. Now when I see someone lost in the world, struggling to find their way, I am immediately filled with compassion for them. I used to just be angry at their choices, the cause of lostness. But Christ in me is making a profound difference. As you encounter the lost and wounded, are you moved with compassion? The challenge for today is to examine our hearts and find how we feel about lost sheep. When we see the rebel, or the wanderer, are we moved with the compassion of Christ? That would be a world-changing event. Compassion thrives when we love in way of the Serving King...

SV

DAY 102

Now Hiring

"Hire for passion and intensity; there is training for everything else."
—*Nolan Bushnell*

Then He said to His disciples, "The harvest is plentiful, but the laborers are few; therefore pray earnestly to the Lord of the harvest to send out laborers into His harvest." (Matthew 9:37-38)

Jobs are a blessing, especially, when we are doing something we love. However, in some instances, we dread going to the same place each day and working the dull nine-to-five. I have discovered the same can be true in our spiritual life. Sometimes we can be excited about the opportunities God gives us, or we can just be going through the motions. And those going through the motions seldom have passion and intensity or pray for the harvest.

Here, in the climax of Jesus teaching on the harvest, He offers a great position: Come work for Me. He suggests there is a huge need for laborers willing to come bring in the harvest; the glorious task of reaping souls for the Kingdom of God.

Jesus gives us two things to consider as we approach the harvest field. First, it is enormous. Everywhere we go, there are souls desperately needing salvation, redemption, and hope. If we live with a heart of compassion, we will see the need for workers to come and reap the harvest. I am amazed that God would choose us to help be the reapers in His harvest. What a privilege to work in His fields.

Second, Jesus is also encouraging us to pray earnestly for workers to come. Wow! We are not the only laborers, but we are recruiters as well! We do not have to stress about doing all the work ourselves. We can call on God with all our hearts to raise up more workers to join us in the fields.

Are we praying for the Kingdom of God to come? Are we praying for the Body of Christ to rise? Are we spreading the Gospel as a worker in God's field? That is the challenge for today! Trust God to bring a harvest, and rejoice that you are not alone in this glorious work. It is a critical task as we love on like the Serving King…
SV

Love Your Work

"Jesus told the disciples not to rejoice in successful service, and yet this seems to be the one thing in which most of us do rejoice. We have the commercial view—so many souls saved and sanctified, thank God, now it is all right."
—Oswald Chambers

And He called to Him His twelve disciples and gave them authority over unclean spirits, to cast them out, and to heal every disease and every affliction.

(Matthew 10:1)

More dangerous to a 'heart after God' is an infatuation with 'God's work', success in the harvest. Lurking, as well, is the 'The Danger of Commercialism' arising in the most subtle of forms as the child trekking after the Serving King begins to crave the sense of accomplishment. Success in the most important of all tasks, the redemption of 'souls', can be an enticing distraction; especially, when God has proclaimed in the early days of conversions, "Job well done, good and faithful servant!" The thrill of new birth goes beyond description.

This becomes even more problematic as those 'saved souls' begin to sing your praises, all in the form of praises to God, but nonetheless striking a chord of accomplishment deep within your soul. It is in those moments you must turn your attention toward God and God alone; else you will soon discover how easily the praise of God can be drowned out by the praise of 'saved souls'. And how equally fast the 'ear' soon begins to tune itself to the praise of those who have genuinely experienced the redemption God has made possible through you. There is great rejoicing in the discovery "...spirits are subject to you."

Follow the instruction of Jesus and resist the temptation to celebrate, especially with others, the successes God brings. Instead, rejoice with God and God alone. Turn your ear to God's praise and resist the temptation to join in the celebration of those who have found redemption in Christ. It is in the moment of success that you must be on your guard to protect yourself from a spirit of 'commercialism' that will ultimately chip away at the foundation of a relationship with God. Beware the danger of success in the things of God. Trek on tuned only to the praise of the Serving King. Such is the way of those who learn to love on in the way of the Serving King...
DM

First Things First

"Faith is taking the first step even when you don't see the whole staircase."
—Martin Luther King Jr.

The twelve Jesus sent out, instructing them, "Go nowhere among the Gentiles and enter no town of the Samaritans, but go rather to the lost sheep of the house of Israel..." (Matthew 10:5-6)

Order matters, sometimes shockingly so; especially as the Kingdom of Heaven arrives. You will be tempted to ask, "What difference does it make who hears the news first?" A reasonable question given our lack of concern regarding order. But order matters in the Kingdom of Heaven. Thus, the command of Jesus to first go to the lost sheep in the House of Israel.

Now in the sunset years of ministry, I find myself wondering about importance of order. Too often in ministry, I was quick to scamper off toward the wounded and broken, moved with compassion, knowing Jesus placed a high priority on the lost. But as I reflect on almost four decades of ministry, I find myself contemplating the command of Jesus, "...go to the lost sheep of Israel." No, not Jerusalem, or the nation of Israel; rather, to my own house of Israel, my own family. Like so many pastors before me, I may have spent too many days away from my own 'house of Israel'.

Thus, the challenge of Jesus to keep 'first things first'. And, for many, family first, your own 'house of Israel', easily falls to second place in the order of priorities. It may be in this moment in time that Jesus says to you, "Go nowhere among the Gentiles..." You will be tempted to argue the point, to insist on the importance of finding the lost sheep. But that is never your concern; it is His. Until He releases you, or possibly sends you, these are the days to make your own 'house of Israel' a top priority.

Rest assured, just because you cannot see the 'whole staircase', does not mean He cannot see it as well. And the Good Shepherd never forgets the 'lost sheep'. But, there are many shepherds trekking after the Serving King. He always sends one of them. In the meantime, hear His command, take it seriously, focus your heart and mind on your own 'house of Israel'. They also need to be loved in the way of the Serving King...
DM

The Workers Temptation...

"The great need for the Christian worker is to be ready to face Jesus Christ at any and every turn...If we are going to be ready for Jesus Christ, we have to stop being religious (that is, using religion as a higher kind of culture) and be spiritually real." —Oswald Chambers

The twelve Jesus sent out, instructing them, "...but go rather to the lost sheep of the house of Israel. And proclaim as you go saying, 'The Kingdom of Heaven is at hand.'" (Matthew 10:6-7)

No worker trekking after the Serving King aspires to be a 'maintenance worker', dedicated to the care and prolongation of the religious culture, frequently called the 'church', or in this case, 'the house of Israel'. The 'church', never to be confused with 'The Church', the Body of Christ, has a way of seducing the 'worker' set on the path of trekking after Jesus. The church is crafty in its seduction, clothing itself in the cares and concerns of the Serving King. Nonetheless, it's more frequently concerned about its own continued viability than the actual 'business' of helping the children of the King to trek closely in His footsteps. Or, more importantly, helping lost children find their way to the King.

But the seduction is deeper yet for that rare worker, the one who finds sustenance for life, food and shelter, from the community of the church. That worker, the pastor, radically depends on the church for life's necessities. So the temptation to embrace the command of Jesus to first go to the 'house of Israel'. But the call is never the last call. It is a starting place, a launching pad, for the work yet still ahead.

Thus, it becomes critical for the 'worker' to pause in their 'work' of religion, and to look around, to see if Jesus is still anywhere near? For if He is gone, then the 'worker' has succumbed to simply 'being religious', has become a 'maintenance worker' prolonging and caring for the 'church', while the authentic Church, the Body of Christ, has continued along the trek, never losing sight of the Serving King, staying close by His side. Then you will remember, "You must also be ready, for the Son of Man is coming at an hour you do not expect." Then the meaning of 'be ready' becomes ever so clear. Never lose sight of the Serving King less you fall into the trap of 'being religious', seduced by the 'religious culture': the 'church'. The 'Church' can always be found only at the side of Jesus. Love on...
DM

Comprehensive Healing

"Do we believe that God can garrison the imagination far beyond where we can go? 'The blood of Jesus Christ cleanseth us from all sin'—if that means in conscious experience only, may God have mercy on us." —Oswald Chambers

"Heal the sick, raise the dead, cleanse the lepers, cast out demons. You received without paying; give without paying." (Matthew 10:8)

Youthfulness provides such innocence, an innocence wanting to believe in the inherent goodness of humanity, all of humanity, including self. However, the journey, a journey all must take, eventually proves innocence wrong, including a slow-to-die hopefulness in self. Slowly comes the recognition self cannot be fixed, nor cleansed, nor healed, nor improved, etc., by self. As all discover at some point, self is crippled, tainted, damaged, ever so slightly or greatly, always enough to distort self in a tragic manner. A single degree off course soon takes you miles from 'who' you intended to be. It is the great tragedy of the human condition.

As innocence dies, so will hope, ultimately enabling you to accept the crippled self, even loving the crippled self; perhaps, even so bold as to declare the crippled self good. However, those trekking after the Serving King discover a new source of 'hope', a source free of the limitations of self, free from the infection of decay, free to be and do in ways that self never could. God, discovered and embraced, set free to heal what only God can heal.. The unthinkable now possible, healing for the crippled self, a new way of being and doing just over the horizon.

Be warned, God intends to fix what really ails the self. That fix will probe and prod you to very core of your being into the whole spirit, soul, and body. As the Spirit of God bores into the very essence of your being, expect moments of discomfort, moments of self-discovery and cleansing, moments of anguish, moments of great joy and, most profoundly, freedom for and from self. A new way of being and doing is ushered in, His way of being and doing. Then, and only then, life authentically begins, liberated from the obsessions of the self-centered self. So we pray, "May the God of peace sanctify you through and through..." Then you will know the joy of loving in the way of the Serving King…
DM

DAY 107

Endless Conversation

"To see and listen to the wicked is already the beginning of wickedness."
—Confucius

"As you enter a house, greet it. And if the house is worthy, let your peace come upon it, but if it is not worthy, let your peace return to you. And if anyone will not receive you or listen to your words, shake off the dust from your feet when you leave that house or town." (Matthew 10:12-14)

Admittedly, the command to "shake off the dust from your feet" sounds profoundly out of character for the Serving King. Abandoning the quest is rarely the offered course of action from the Serving King. Nonetheless, there comes those moments in life when a change of course is needed simply because the timing or current course of action is fruitless. The wisdom to know when that moment has arrived is difficult to secure. Still, the command of the Serving King is abundantly clear. This is not the time nor place for continued engagement. Leave while you can.

Tragically, the 'foe', having long mastered the art of wearing 'sheep's clothing', the ravenous wolf, wields a deadly weapon: unproductive conversation. And conversation, deceptively engaging, distracts the noble missionary endlessly. Round and round it goes, hour after hour, day after day. It is ultimate sheep's clothing. A seemingly harmless passing of the hours.

It is the 'great distraction' for the well-intentioned, 'noble' missionary, so wanting to please God by caring for God's children. Answering every question, soon reduced to nothing more than a talk show host. And the 'wolf', the 'false prophet', dressed in the nobility of 'sheep's clothing', the conversationalist, cheers on the distracted talker, delighted to capture them with little more than conversation.

Beware the 'great distraction', so easily entangling the 'call' of the Serving King, rendering the noble missionary another talker in the crowd of sympathetic hearts. Listening to the wicked is indeed already the beginning of wickedness; not because what is being conversed about is inherently evil, but because it keeps the Gospel locked in the cycle of unproductive conversation. Sometimes loving like the Serving King mandates a change of location, a change of venue. Leave while you can, and look for another to love on in the ways of the Serving King…
DM

DAY 108

Wolves

"Liberty for wolves is death to the lambs." —Isaiah Berlin

"Behold, I am sending you out as sheep in the midst of wolves, so be wise as serpents and innocent as doves. Beware of men, for they will deliver you over to courts and flog you in their synagogues..." (Matthew 10:21)

Sometimes the issue is even more significant than wrong time, wrong place; instead, it is an issue of danger from prolonged exposure to inappropriate people, inappropriate ideas, wolves even. This is no mere distraction by conversation; more seriously, danger lurks as wolves in sheep's clothing plot the missionary's ultimate demise. And, in this instance, the Serving King has other plans in mind.

Moderns, long adjusted to living in the land of the free, have long forgotten, if they ever knew, the dangers of proclaiming the Good News of the Gospel. Accustomed to a culture established on the values of the Serving King, liberty taken for granted, conversations abound. But change is in the air. The values of the Kingdom of God, once a mainstay of American culture, no longer govern, no longer provide the guarantee of liberty and justice for all. There is a new law in the land, the law of Political Correctness, and whoa to the sheep who dare to voice an unpolitically-correct idea. The wolves will soon chase down even the fastest of prey.

So the warning of Jesus to those in the land of the wolves; especially wolves dressed in sheep's clothing. Take seriously the need to keep moving. This is not the time for one final stand. This is the time to keep moving farther down the line. Rest assured, the wolves will keep moving as well. They are accustomed to chasing down prey. They will find you soon enough.

But the wolves can be outwitted. It is their proverbial 'achilles heal'. Keep your wits about you as you move quickly down the line. There are still other towns, other villages, waiting for the Good News of the Gospel. Today is not the day for your journey to end. Be wise as serpents as you love on in the ways of Serving King.

DM

DAY 109

Reflection

"You are the only Bible some unbelievers will ever read." —John MacArthur

"The student is not above the teacher, nor a servant above his master. It is enough for students to be like their teachers, and servants like their masters. If the head of the house has been called Beelzebul, how much more the members of his household!" (Matthew 10:24-25)

Bill Hendren was a Christian man who lived in Mexico, MO. He was tall in stature; a strong and built man, and a man of many trades. He built houses, tended gardens, and worked with his hands. He loved his family, his community, his church and, most importantly, God. When he passed, people came from near and far to celebrate their friend and tell stories about his life. Over and over again, family heard of how his life of love and kindness led person after person to know Jesus Christ as their Lord and Savior.

Bill was not a man who lived a perfect life. In fact, he lived alongside the world for many years. He had his struggles and vices. One night, a friend invited Bill and his wife to a tent revival service where his life was changed forever. That night, he heard about a God who loved him and a Savior who had paid the price for his sin and had come to set him free. With those words, he stood up in a crowd and made his way to an altar where he prayed for salvation. He laid down his vices that night and picked up a brand-new life in the Lord Jesus. In a moment of time, he became a follower of the Serving King.

That night everything changed. When you looked upon the face of Bill Hendren, you saw a reflection of Jesus. He was kinder and gentler. He loved with a pure love that could only come from God Almighty.

Who is your master? Who do others see and hear when they encounter you? As we live in a world of sheep amongst wolves, may the love of Christ shine forth to those around us. May someone know Him because they know you. Like Bill, may there be many who come to know Jesus simply because of their connection to you, your simple invitation. Love on in the way of the Serving King…

ME

When the Light Comes On

"Courage is being scared to death... and saddling up anyway." —John Wayne

"So have no fear of them, for nothing is covered that will not be revealed, or hidden that will not be known." (Matthew 10:26)

I remember lying in my bed and flinching at every sound. Against my parents' wishes, I watched a horror movie not intended for my 10-year-old eyes, and I was paying the price! There was a scene in the movie where a teen who had been transformed into a vampire levitated up to a large second story storm window and scratched on the glass. This scratching awakened his younger brother who opened the window and let him in. Of course, the younger brother was bitten and became a vampire! There I was, lying just below a similar storm window in my East Texas home, with the branches of the large tree directly outside my window reacting to the high winds by making the same "vampire" scratching noises! I was petrified.

Then, something amazing happened: I got up and turned on the light. I confess that I slept with it on all night, consistently looking out the window making sure that the scraping noise was a tree and not a vampire. The next morning, I got up, went outside, and stood next to the tree. It didn't look scary at all. It was rather old and had lost most of its leaves. The light revealed I did not need to be afraid. After a short while, I no longer allowed the tree's scraping to scare me. I boldly turned off my light and calmly listened to the wind and rain as I fell asleep.

Jesus knew that His disciples would have scary times. These times would include opposition and, for some, even death! However, in this passage, Jesus reminds them, and us, that we do not need to fear. He reminds us that God has a way of caring for even the most helpless and vulnerable of creatures (sparrows, for example, in 10:29), and is, therefore, more than capable of caring for us. God's protection empowers us to proclaim and live His message with boldness and confidence in His care. Jesus would go on to prove that not even the most frightening of things—death—has the power to stop His work as we keep loving like the Serving King...
CC

DAY 111

Breaking the Huddle

"Finding good players is easy. Getting them to play as a team is another story."
—Casey Stengel

"What I tell you in the dark, say in the light, and what you hear whispered, proclaim on the housetops." (Matthew 10:27)

I never played high school football, but I grew up playing a lot of playground football. So, I learned the importance of the huddle: moving back several yards from the ball and giving instructions to all the receivers, sometimes drawing out the plays in the dirt. The huddle was an exciting place, full of anticipation and dreaming of the big play that could break the game open and bring us to victory. But, of course, we couldn't stay in the huddle forever, as exciting as it may have been. If we stayed too long in the huddle, we would risk "delay of game" complaints from the other team and be penalized. When we broke from the huddle to lining up for the play, it was time to put the play in motion. The huddle was secretive, but then the play would be executed for all to see.

Jesus valued times of quiet interaction with His disciples. They, too, enjoyed the pleasure of His company as they sat together as 'the Twelve' and explored the mysteries of the Kingdom of God, conversing with the Messiah Himself. However, they were not called to simply huddle together quietly. They were called to execute the play! What was whispered to them in those quiet moments with the Savior was meant to be then "proclaimed from the housetops" (10:27). This was so the whole world could see the love and mercy of God made known through the coming of this same Jesus, who was not only their Lord and Savior, but was and is the Savior of the whole world. There's a time to huddle together in intimate connection with the Savior. But there is also a time to break free and move into a lost and dying world as bearers of the hope that is in Jesus Christ as we keep loving like the Serving King…
CC

The Flow of Confession

"Sacrifice, discipline and prayer are essential. We gain strength through God's word. We receive grace from the sacrament. And when we fumble due to sin - and it's gonna happen - confession puts us back on the field. " —Lou Holtz

"So everyone who acknowledges Me before men, I will also acknowledge before my Father in Heaven, but whoever denies Me before men, I will also deny before My Father who is in heaven." (Matthew 10:32-33)

Have we ever taken a moment and asked ourselves, who do we communicate (confess) with our lives each day? When we speak? When we respond (or react)? With our attitudes? With our forgiveness (or bitterness)? With our love? Whom do people hear when they are watching us live out our lives?

Jesus is very poignant: you confess Me before people, I will confess you before the Father. If people hear Me in your verbiage, I will verbalize how proud I am of you before the Father. If they see My love in your life, I will scream My love for you. If people see My character and integrity in your life, I will send a screen shot to the Angels and those who have gone before you. It is vital that we communicate God in every area of our lives, so God will communicate us before the Father, when it counts.

When Jon Huss was about to be burned at the stake, he was given multiple opportunities to recant and deny his theological underpinnings- but he would not. When they went to tie him to the stake, he told the guards not to bother; he was proud to die for the name of Jesus Christ. That is confession.

It doesn't have to be that drastic: we can confess by our kindness to someone we would not normally associate with. Our confession could be forgiving someone who has wronged us in the past. Our confession could be a quietness, when the whole world around us is burning in anger and hatred. Or, our confession could be having the face of an Angel, when the crowd has lied about you and has decided to kill you- like Stephen.

How will we confess Christ today? It may be a planned confession, or maybe a situation will arise providing an opportunity to show the love and mercy of God. The most important thing is that we are prepared for and watch for opportunities as we love on like the Serving King.

JL

Costly Grace

"Such grace is costly because it calls us to follow, and it is grace because it calls us to follow Jesus Christ. It is costly because it costs a man his life, and it is grace because it gives a man the only true life."— Dietrich Bonhoeffer

"I have not come to bring peace, but a sword. For I have come to set a man against his father, and a daughter against her mother, and a daughter-in-law against her mother-in-law; and one's foes will be members of one's own household." (Matthew 10:34-36)

This is one of those passages that people struggle with, and understandably so. Is this really what Jesus was all about? We have enough division in the world, why would Jesus seemingly endorse more and deeper divisions than already exist? In addition, a Christian home should not be the place of such division. We want to have homes where grace and peace are the hallmarks, not division and strife. Does Jesus really endorse conflict here? It is natural that this passage confuses us.

We should remember that this is one of those places where the 2000 years and the cultural divide between ancient Israel and today can lead us to a wrong conclusion. The Gospel of Matthew was written in a time when one's role in a family and the larger society meant everything. One did not seek to amass wealth as a reward as much as the accumulation of honor. One gained honor by living the role set for you by one's family and the larger community.

What we tend to forget is that if one decided to follow Christ, that was more than just an individual decision. It was a decision that impacted the whole family and determined one's standing within the community. Jesus was looking ahead to the cultural impact of becoming a Christian, and recognizing that if one is going to follow Christ, it may cause a divide within the family. This division is not the goal but might be the natural consequence of following Christ. We have similar concerns today. If we are a part of a Christian family and live in the U.S., it is hard to imagine these words of Jesus. Yet, the call to follow Christ may come between us and a job, friends, or goals in life. Our call to follow Christ is not a call to make Christ a part of our life, but our whole life. When we do, the cost of following may impact the things that we love most. In the first century that would have meant the family. We may not know what impact it will make, but the call of Christ still impacts lives today. Love on like the Serving King...
DW

DAY 114

Priorities and Choices

"Desires dictate our priorities, priorities shape our choices, and choices determine our actions." —Dallin H. Oakst

Whoever loves father or mother more than Me is not worthy of Me, and whoever loves son or daughter more than Me is not worthy of Me. And whoever does not take his cross and follow Me is not worthy of Me. Whoever finds his life will lose it, and whoever loses his life for My sake will find it. (Matthew 10:37-39)

Often, Jesus makes difficult statements that seem to be in conflict with what He has said at other times. This one is clearly one of those statements. He has criticized the Pharisees and Scribes in Matthew 15 for manufacturing ways to void this law requiring the caring for their father and mother. Here He seems to contradict this commandment.

Some of my best thinking is done while I walk my wife's dog, Tino. While I was walking him one day, God gave me a new insight into this statement of Jesus'. At least, it was new to me. As I thought about it, I came to realize that we are making this same decision often in our lives. While we love our parents, we frequently bring other things into our lives that may seem like we love them less. When I went to college, I left my parents, actually they drove me to California where the college was located. We were separated for the entire school year, and after that, we never spent more than a few weeks in each other's company. When I married Cheryl, it was an even more permanent separation. While I was still a part of the family, I had a new family that took priority over my parents. None of these choices on my part indicated a lessening of my love for my parents. They simply indicated that additional priorities were now a part of my life.

In this passage, Jesus is not calling for a radical separation of parents from children. He is calling for an elevation of our allegiance to Him. To make Him first place in our lives. Perhaps, now is a good time to examine the priorities in your life. Where does your husband or wife and family fit into your life? How much of your time is occupied in work and recreation? What are you doing to benefit the needy or the community in general? And, most important, what are you doing that reflects the Serving King's love in your life?

DS

Rewarding Hospitality

"Hospitality exists when you believe that the other person is on your side."
—*Danny Meyer*

"Whoever receives you receives Me, and whoever receives Me receives Him who sent Me. The one who receives a prophet because he is a prophet will receive a prophet's reward, and the one who receives a righteous person because he is a righteous person will receive a righteous person's reward. And whoever gives one of these little ones even a cup of cold water because he is a disciple, truly, I say to you, he will by no means lose his reward." (Matthew 10:40-42)

Jesus' discussion of receiving others and gaining rewards seems almost like it shouldn't be in the Bible. Sure, we should receive His servants and offer aid and compassion to those in need. But if we should do the right thing no matter what the result, it seems crass to talk in terms of rewards for those actions. Shouldn't we do good just for the sake of doing good?

If we look back just a little, we remember the harsh verses earlier in this chapter of Matthew. Jesus challenges His hearers to leave families, if necessary, to follow Him. This somewhat vague passage about receiving reward is here, because it comes on the heels of the warning that following God may result in great sacrifice. Perhaps, His hearers were wondering what could possibly motivate someone to follow when the cost could be so great. Jesus does not hide the difficulties of a life chasing God, but He does not leave followers in despair either.

In these verses, Jesus offers a refocus to what God gives. The rewards that follow when we receive those who are serving God are good. We receive good things when we receive not only those that Christ sends but also their message. Jesus also goes beyond just welcoming those with a message to offer, of receiving those who are clearly servants of God. He also reminds us that even when there is no reward on earth, when the person we serve can offer nothing in return, God repays us with heavenly rewards. While the cost may be immense, they are greatly outweighed. The promise of God is greater. The richness of relationship with our Creator is greater. These verses are not here to motivate necessarily, but to encourage us. May we live well knowing that while the things of earth, even our most dear relationships can fade or crumble, what God gives can never diminish or be taken away. Love on like the Serving King...
RS

DAY 116

Finished?

"Suffering is but another name for the teaching of experience, which is the parent of instruction and the schoolmaster of life." —Horace

When Jesus had finished instructing His twelve disciples, He went on from there to teach and preach in their cities. (Matthew 11:1)

He was finished. You must understand that fact if the full meanings of His actions are to be understood. Jesus invested His three years of ministry in the training of twelve disciples. His training covered everything from attitudes and relationships to eschatology and perseverance. His training was practical and inspiring, and sometimes difficult to understand and hard to accept. He was obviously preparing them for His eventual departure: preparing them to go into all the world and make disciples.

And as with any good trainer, He prepared an opportunity for His trainees to practice what they were being taught. He gave them their assignment; providing them with all the instructions they needed, defined their desired outcomes, and sent them out. But what happens next is not what you would have expected. This is the point we must hear the words, "when He was finished." For you see, when He was finished, He began working.

Let's face it; the disciples weren't exactly easy students, and He had to be exhausted from the training process. He had invested His whole being into teaching them. His tireless efforts to train, guide, and equip them had undoubtedly taken a toll on His body, mind, and spirit. Here was His opportunity to rest while they practiced. Every professor has done it. Every trainer has too. Once the assignment is given, they take a break while the students/trainees complete the assignment. But not Jesus!

Instead of yielding to His emotional and physical tiredness, He sets out on His own teaching and preaching tour. Why? The answer is found in Peter's description of God, "not wishing that any should perish, but that all should reach repentance" (2 Peter 3:9). His very being is defined by His desire for men and women to repent and follow Him. So, He doesn't take a vacation while the disciples complete their training assignment; instead, He invests that time in reaching more people with the Gospel. Love drives us in ways nothing else can. Keep loving…
DS

DAY 117

You are it!

"The very essence of leadership is that you have to have vision. You can't blow an uncertain trumpet." —Theodore Hesburgh

"Are You the One who is to come, or shall we look for another?" And Jesus answered them, "Go and tell John what you hear and see: the blind receive their sight and the lame walk, lepers are cleansed and the deaf hear, and the dead are raised up, and the poor have Good News preached to them. And blessed is the one who is not offended by Me." (Matthew 11:2-6)

Absolutely, no doubt about it! Are you sure? I think so. This kind of uncertain faith seems to describe John the Baptist when he asks, "Are you the One who is to come, or shall we look for another?" John's earlier conversation at the baptism of Jesus had left the impression that John may have known who Jesus was: "I need to be baptized by You" (Matthew 3:14).

Reading the Book of John also leaves you with this same impression, "John bore witness about Him, and cried out, "This was He of whom I said, He who comes after me ranks before me, because He was before me."" But something has changed since these earlier times. What was it?

The answer is most likely found in verse 2, "Now when John…in prison…" You see, bad things happen to good people! And the faith of good people sometimes wobbles in bad times. Job's faith certainly did as he faced his accusers. Some of the Psalms that David penned revealed his struggles. And it's likely such a struggle is seen here in the heart of John. Does John have a spiritual problem? No. He is experiencing the limitations of an earthly body and mind. In all likelihood, we all have or will experience similar doubts and faith challenges when we face extreme difficulties.

Christ's answer to combat John's doubts; go and describe to John what you are seeing. Tell him about blind individuals who now see. Describe the cripples who are now bounding about. Tell him about the lepers and the deaf who now have perfect skin and perfect hearing. And, of course, how the dead are now enjoying life and the company of their family and friends. In other words, describe to John the power you have seen Me demonstrate. God's lack of intervention in our lives is not a reason to doubt His power or His love. Remember this key principle: When we don't understand why He has not intervened in our situation, we can still trust in who He is and in His heart? Loving like the Serving King liberates us to stay the course in times of uncertainty…
DS

DAY 118

The Paradox...

"The paradox is that God must destroy in us, all illusions of righteousness before he can make us righteous..." —Martin Luther

"Truly, I say to you, among those born of women there has arisen no one greater than John the Baptist. Yet the one who is least in the Kingdom of Heaven is greater than he." (Matthew 11:11-12)

The temptation, for those so inclined, lures the novice, amateurs, in being good, to seek personal righteousness as a means of right standing before God. Some soon begin to rest in their goodness, even pondering the possibility of being good; or at least, better than most. But, better than most, good as that may be, is a long way from righteousness, God's way of being and doing. John the Baptist provides case in point. So the paradox begins; the better one appears to be, the further one feels from the righteousness of God so desperately sought after. Another way is needed.

One alternative, painless and expedient, a simple lowering of the standard, a being and doing easily within reach of the many, a standard the crowds cheer with delight. The many, sensing His way of being and doing beyond reach, lessen the standard, making good attainable for the least among us. Another way is needed.

Righteousness, God's way of being and doing, is the road less traveled, and not because none have so desired; rather, simply because the doing is utterly dependent on being, neither of which comes naturally to those chasing after the Serving King. But there is one, Jesus the Christ, whose being and doing reflects the righteousness of God, a good far exceeding the efforts of the many. In Him, the Serving King, God shows His righteousness in flesh and blood. And this righteousness of God can only be manifest in the final dimension of self-sacrifice, a complete surrender to the will of God, regardless of the cost, in every 'present time'.

And once seen, comprehended, the gig is up, the illusion utterly destroyed. There can be no 'righteousness' apart from His. Thus, the finality of the paradox. Only in Him can the righteousness of God be found. But it can never be found until every illusion of righteousness is gone. Love on in the way of the Serving King...
DM

DAY 119

Dare To Hear

"Here in America we are descended in blood and in spirit from revolutionists and rebels - men and women who dare to dissent from accepted doctrine. As their heirs, may we never confuse honest dissent with disloyal subversion."
—Dwight D. Eisenhower

For all the Prophets and the Law prophesied until John, and if you are willing to accept, He is Elijah who is to come. He who has ears to hear, let him hear.
(Matthew 11:15)

Revolutionists and rebels, from Abraham to Paul, George Washington to Dwight D. Eisenhower, all have a common thread running through them: They have heard God. And with hearing God often comes the need for honest dissent, a breaking free from the Law, yesterday's ways of being and doing, long practiced by trusted family and friends. But dissent always comes with a price, expensive and demanding, requiring faithful chasing on the heels of the Serving King. He leads into tomorrow's promises, away from yesterday's heard God, instructions for yesterday's moment, now with a life of their own…

The many, terrified of new ways of being and doing, close ranks, demanding ever-increasing loyalty to the old ways, insisting the inheritance will only go to those who stay the course. But they are wrong, very wrong, wandering around in yesterday's heard God. And you are not engaged in disloyal subversion, rather honest dissent, mandated in the life of those who have heard God in this present moment, those who must abandon all previous claims, stepping into the promise of today's heard God.

So comes the promise of faith, fluidity mandated for those intent on chasing after the Serving King, an inheritance for all who dare to step into today's heard God. By definition, people of faith are always revolutionist and rebels, "…men and women who dare to dissent from accepted doctrine." We are the children of Abraham, revolutionists and rebels, hearing the today's voice of God, leaving behind the comfort zones of old, boldly seeking the promise of God in the present moment. But change rarely comes cheap and few are those willing to pay the price of the revolution, to embrace the cross of the Serving King. John the Baptist paid the price. Many are willing to go to war, but few, very few, are willing to embrace His way of being and doing, the way of the cross. Love on in the way of the Serving King…
DM

Can You Still Imagine?

"Is your imagination stayed on God or is it starved? The starvation of the imagination is one of the most fruitful sources of exhaustion and sapping in a worker's life. If you have never used your imagination to put yourself before God, begin to do it now." —Oswald Chambers

"He who has ears to hear, let him hear." (Matthew 11:15)

Imagination for many trekking after God suggests a negative connotation, implying not real or make pretend, rather than the crucial ability to hear and see God in the mundane and profane. You will have to grow up and learn how to use your imagination again, as powerfully as a child, if you are to succeed in seeing and hearing as Jesus called us to. It is only the 'imagination' that will enable you to 'see and hear' the very essence of God, imprinted deep into the 'mind' of the 'seer', the one who can still 'imagine'.

This will not come easy for most, having lost the ability to imagine our way into the very presence of the Living God. Ours is a culture of science, with its rigid and stifling rules, insisting only that which can be measured and measured repeatedly be given any attention. The ability to imagine is forbidden, relegated to the land of make pretend, robbing the child of God of the Creator's tremendous gift to those who are willing to use it, explore it, embrace it, and allow imagination to usher in reality and life in ways that the measurable never can. So Chambers warns us of the dangers of a 'starved imagination', weak and feeble, unable to usher us into the very presence of the Living God.

Even in this godless land of the unimagined dominated by the demigods of science, the artists among us valiantly seek to keep the imagination alive, vibrant, capable of transcending the mundane of that which can be measured, ushering the child of God into the very essence of God, into the very presence of the Living God. Imagination is that pathway, gifted by God, enabling all who are willing to explore it to find the very essence of the Living God. You will have to shake off the mundane world of science to get there, but it can be done. "If you have never used your imagination to put yourself before God, begin to do it now." Those who hear soon learn how to love on in the ways of the Serving King...
DM

The Gospel in People

"We have two ears and one mouth so that we can listen twice as much as we speak." —Epictetus

"But to what will I compare this generation? It is like children sitting in the marketplaces and calling to one another, 'We played the flute for you, and you did not dance; we wailed, and you did not mourn.' For John came neither eating nor drinking, and they say, 'He has a demon'; the Son of Man came eating and drinking, and they say, 'Look, a glutton and a drunkard, a friend of tax collectors and sinners!' Yet wisdom is vindicated by her deeds."

(Matthew 11:16-19)

Do you know anyone who is never satisfied? Their coffee is always either too hot or too cold, too bitter or too sweet, too weak or too strong. Their work is either too boring or too busy, too easy or too stressful. They think everything should happen in a very particular way, and they dismiss whatever doesn't match those expectations.

This is how Jesus described the people of His day. He compared His own ministry to that of John the Baptist, saying that the two of them shared the same Gospel message but proclaimed it in different ways, yet the people were unwilling to accept the Good News from either of them. When John preached, he did so as a fervently Jewish ascetic who maintained a strict diet and separated himself from any of the pleasures of the world (see Matt. 3:4–5), yet the people rejected him as demonic. When Jesus preached, He did so by entering into the lives of people, serving and healing them as He ate and drank with them, yet the people rejected Him as too worldly. Because neither of them matched the people's expectations, the people dismissed their message about the coming Kingdom of God.

In my life, I've found that it's easy for me to find a reason to discount another person's perspective. If they come from a theological background that I generally don't agree with, or if they use language that I don't like, or if they are too old or too young… if I can find any reason whatsoever, I tend to disregard their opinions. After all, it's far easier for me to ignore them than it is to wrestle with their thoughts that challenge my own perceptions.

But is it possible that they are presenting a Gospel message I need to hear? I will never know if I refuse to consider it. And I think Jesus would probably encourage us to listen to people—even those we would rather disregard—to find the Kingdom of God in them. Listening is a first step in learning how to love in the ways of the Serving King…

RG

DAY 122

Without Excuse

"Look up at the stars and not down at your feet. Try to make sense of what you see, and wonder about what makes the universe exist. Be curious." —*Stephen Hawking*

"For if the mighty works done in you had been done in Sodom, it would have remained until this day. But I tell you that it will be more tolerable on the day of judgment for the land of Sodom than for you." (Matthew 11:20-24)

It is amazing how many, regardless of who they are, can physically see, and emotionally be touched or intellectually note that something beyond the 'normal' has happened, and still write it off as coincidence. Recognizing the activity of God never crosses their minds. Yet, people call tornados and cyclones the 'finger of God.' Hurricanes and earthquakes the 'hand of God.' Typhoons and windstorm's the 'force of God.' However, these same people will never call creation the 'handiwork of God.'

In our passage, Jesus is making a statement of great importance. He speaks of 'mighty works' done in front of all, and yet the people would not recognize the hand of God. He began to denounce the cities where most of His mighty works had been done, because they would not repent. A pronounced rebuke from the Lord against all those who can plainly see yet blatantly reject the 'handiwork of God.' Those who see without seeing.

Romans 1:18-21 declares: "For the wrath of God is revealed from heaven against all ungodliness and unrighteousness of men, who by their unrighteousness suppress the truth. For what can be known about God is plain to them because God has shown it to them. For His invisible attributes, namely, His eternal power and divine nature, have been clearly perceived, ever since the creation of the world, in the things that have been made. So, they are without excuse. For although they knew God, they did not honor Him as God or give thanks to Him, but they became futile in their thinking, and their foolish hearts were darkened."

It is foolish to reject what is plainly understood as being beyond our ability to comprehend. To reject God, His handiwork, and His salvation that is given through His Only Son Jesus is foolishness. I would recommend accepting the great works done through Jesus and find the life. Those who see have discovered the path toward loving like the Serving King…

TM

More than Miracles

"How quickly we forget God's great deliverances in our lives. How easily we take for granted the miracles he performed in our past." —David Wilkerson

Then He began to denounce the cities where most of His mighty works had been done, because they did not repent. "Woe to you, Chorazin! Woe to you, Bethsaida! For if the mighty works done in you had been done in Tyre and Sidon, they would have repented long ago in sackcloth and ashes.

(Matthew 11:20-21)

One of the natural desires for many Christians, or people of any "faith," for that matter, is to experience something supernatural. To see a miracle that will leave no doubt as to the existence of God and the validity of their faith. I've both heard and said many times, "If only I could have been lucky enough to have seen the waters part, or the dead raised."

Throughout the Book of John, Jesus often expresses irritation at the request to "perform a sign" in order that they might believe. Jesus would bristle at this need for a miracle, and it wasn't until recently in my life that I began to understand why. Jesus said the greatest commandments were to love God with all your heart, soul, strength, and mind, and the second was like it, to love your neighbor as yourself. Even for one who doesn't believe in a God, it should be clear that the teaching to love your neighbor as yourself would transform the world if lived out by all. The fact is Jesus taught love, the highest level of love, and the truth of love should be so obvious that no miracles need accompany it to provide validity.

Therefore, when Jesus took the time to perform His miracles, they weren't so much to provide faith, they were to show the lack thereof. Jesus knew that if people couldn't clearly see the validity of love, then even signs and miracles would not be enough to convince a person.

In this passage today, Jesus expresses clear frustration with the towns He had performed the most miracles in. They not only missed His great message of love, they also failed to see the miracles as verification that, perhaps, He might have known what He was talking about. Blessed are those who do not see and still believe and love on like the Serving King...

WH

DAY 124

Definitions

"When you find your definitions in God, you find the very purpose for which you were created." —Ravi Zacharias

At that time Jesus declared, "I thank you, Father, Lord of Heaven and Earth, that You have hidden these things from the wise and understanding and revealed them to little children; yes, Father, for such was Your gracious will. All things have been handed over to Me by my Father, and no one knows the Son except the Father, and no one knows the Father except the Son and anyone to whom the Son chooses to reveal Him." (Matthew 11:25-27)

My family has a black lab named Nelly. We got Nelly as a puppy and she was our first "child." Black labs are simultaneously as dumb as rocks and geniuses. It's science (don't Google it). When Nelly was just a few months old, she had a tendency to chew up pretty much anything she could get her paws on. So, when we would leave the house, we often tried to come up with clever ways to keep her contained so that she didn't end up digesting something very dangerous. She didn't know better, and we were trying to protect her. Inevitably, we would come home to discover that she had "Houdinied" a way to escape the fortress that we had created with our furniture and other household items.

Where am I going with this? Back to the beginning. Counter to popular beliefs, the original sin of humanity in the Garden wasn't simply taking a bite of bad fruit. Eating from the tree of "Knowledge of Good and Evil" was an act of choosing to define good and evil apart from God's definition and plan for humanity. This is the same choice that we make every day. Do we define good and evil on our own, or do we follow God's definition?

Just like my puppy Nelly, sometimes we're too smart for our own good and we manage to get out and destroy things. We, as humanity, have chosen to define good and evil, instead of following the God that cares for us and places restrictions on us out of love and concern for our own good. In this passage, Jesus is telling us the gift is childlike faith and what it means to blindly follow God's call on our lives. Thankfully, He tells us how to do that in verse 27; when we follow Jesus, we follow God. When we seek after Him, we are surrendering our definition of good and evil and submitting ourselves to His! Loving like the Serving King unleashes His way of being and doing into a broken world longing to be loved...

RA

DAY 125

A Gentle Yoke...

"'Whom the Lord loveth, He chasteneth.' How petty our complaining is! Our Lord begins to bring us into the place where we can have communion with Him, and we groan and say—'Oh Lord, let me be like other people!' Jesus is asking us to take one end of the yoke—'My yoke is easy, get alongside Me and we will pull together.'"—Oswald Chambers

"Take My yoke upon you, and learn from Me, for I am gentle and lowly in heart, and you will find rest for your souls. For My yoke is easy, and My burden is light." (Matthew 11:29)

It is a sobering reality when the child trekking after the King suddenly hears the suggestion, rather, command, to pick up the yoke of the Serving King. But understand this 'picking up of the yoke' is not to assist Jesus in pulling the load; rather, it is to learn how to walk as Jesus, to pull the load. It is important to comprehend what this yoke actually is. Simply, it is learning to think and act as Jesus thinks and acts.

It is in learning to think and act like Jesus that you will be tempted to say, "Oh Lord, let me be like other people!" However, Jesus is not like other people nor will He allow those who are yoked with Him to be like other people. You cannot walk 'yoked' to the Jesus and walk any way but His. That is the whole purpose of the yoke as the two must function as one. You must learn His cadence and pace. It is in the experience of yokedness that you discover in an even more profound way: His ways are not your ways.

Yet, Jesus is forthright in reminding the child trekking after the King that His way of being is not difficult, to the contrary, "For Yy yoke is easy and My burden is light" (Matthew 11:30). But, and this is critical to understand, His way is different, radically different, than how you have lived before. You will be tempted to suggest different is hard, burdensome, and problematic for you. It is not. His way is simply different. A decision will have to be made. Will you stay yoked to Jesus?

Then, some days into yokedness, that moment of blissful discovery as you remain in His yoke, walking with Him, side by side, step by step, His way instead of your way, mile after mile...He is carrying the burden. Then, you understand His concept of 'shared yoke' is nothing like yours. His way is to carry the burden, while you walk and learn in the way of love...

DM

Danger! Work at Your Own Risk!

"Anybody can observe the Sabbath, but making it holy surely takes the rest of the week." —Alice Walker

At that time Jesus went through the grain fields on the Sabbath. His disciples were hungry, and they began to pluck heads of grain and to eat. But when the Pharisees saw it, they said to Him, "Look, Your disciples are doing what is not lawful to do on the Sabbath." (Matthew 12:1-2)

Exodus 35:2 says, "Six days work shall be done, but on the seventh day you shall have a Sabbath of solemn rest, holy to the Lord. Whoever does any work on it shall be put to death." This commandment of the Lord is clear and not up for debate or revocation. But, the interpretation of said Scripture is often up for discussion.

In today's selected Scripture, Jesus and the disciples are enjoying a quiet and relaxing Sabbath walking through some grain fields. I wonder if it was a beautiful day. I wonder if there were any clouds in the sky and a gentle breeze. I wonder if it was on their minds that if they pluck some grain to nourish themselves, they could be put to death. I wonder if they felt in mortal danger for committing such a heinous crime.

And to make matters worse, they did it with Jesus fully knowing and fully present of such an atrocious betrayal of the law! Then I asked myself, "Why did Jesus tell the story of David and the Bread of Presence?" I believe the Pharisees would have known this story and, thus, this situation became a teachable moment for the disciples. I believe Jesus wanted to show the disciples that the intent of the law was to draw God's children closer to Him out of obedience and not just to scare them into obedience. You see, the Pharisees were focused solely on catching Jesus in the crosshairs of semantics. By the letter of the law as written, the disciples were breaking the law and deserved death. But, "…for Jesus, David's eating of the Bread of Presence suggests that human need can at times overrule ritual prohibition" (Baker's Evangelical Dictionary of Biblical Theology). Focus on obedience to the law of Christ which is a law of relationship, not a law of rituals! Relationship is the way of loving in the way of the Serving King…
JP

Son of HuMANity!

"Even very ordinary people, upon closer examination, can often look extraordinary." —Holly Hunter

"I tell you, something greater than the temple is here. And if you had known what this means, 'I desire mercy, and not sacrifice,' you would not have condemned the guiltless. For the Son of Man is Lord of the Sabbath."

(Matthew 12:8)

In yesterday's devotion, we discovered a relationship with Jesus is far more desired than any ritual or sacrifice we can offer Him, even going to church! Jesus states, "For the Son of Man is the Lord of the Sabbath."

There are two questions I want to bring to light. First, what does Jesus mean when He says He is the "Son of Man"? Second, what does He mean when He says he is "Lord of the Sabbath"? I will focus on the former question today. From www.Christianity.com, the author states when speaking about Son of Man, "The more sophisticated and important historical insight is that the term 'Son of Man' doesn't merely align Him with humanity. It is probably taken from Daniel 7. And if you read that chapter, you'll see that the Son of Man is a very exalted figure: not just a human figure but an exalted figure. It was Jesus' favorite self-designation." If you do a study of the term 'Son of Man' in the Gospels, you'll see that He didn't refer to Himself most often as Son of God, but as Son of Man. He said things like, "The Son of Man came not to be served but to serve and to give His life as a ransom for many" (Mark 10:45).

He calls Himself Son of Man very often, and this is significant as it appears Jesus was attempting to further align Himself with us, plain ordinary folks, as opposed to the Divine, which He was fully. Jesus was one of us, fully frail, fully prone to temptation and sin, yet, He did not sin. If Jesus desired to fully align Hmself with us, humanity, will you fully align yourself with Him, Son of HuMANity? It's your choice. Choose Jesus and then love like the Serving King...

JP

The Father and Son are Equal!

"If you don't take a Sabbath, something is wrong. You're doing too much, you're being too much in charge. You've got to quit, one day a week, and just watch what God is doing when you're not doing anything." —Eugene H. Peterson

"For the Son of Man is Lord of the Sabbath." (Matthew 12:1-8)

Yesterday, you learned about the Son of Man, the Son of HuMANity. Today, we will focus on Jesus' words when He says He is "Lord of the Sabbath" or Lord of the day of rest. In order to understand this Scripture, Lord must be defined. According to www.christiancourier.com, "Lord reflects the original term YHWH (found 6,823 times)." So, you will notice in today's Scripture Lord is spelled with all lowercase letters. This is significant if we are to understand and interpret this selected Scripture and all of Scripture when Lord or lord are used in this fashion. When Scripture uses "Lord" with the "L" capitalized, the meaning changes thus the interpretation changes.

The term derives from a root suggesting 'sovereign, strength, or power.' In the selected verse, Lord is used the previous way referring to YHWH, the creator. Is Jesus making Himself equal to the Father? If He's Lord of the Sabbath, He is Lord of the seventh day, the day of rest. And if the Father ordained the day of rest, then Jesus is, in fact, equating Himself with the Father, not as the first person of the Trinity, but in role and presence. I am convinced this is why Jesus said in Matthew 12:6, "I tell you, something greater than the temple is here." He was referring to Himself. He is greater than the temple!

When Matthew penned those words "lord of the Sabbath", he indeed was saying Jesus is the something greater. He has the authority granted to Him to be the God of the day of rest. Jesus rules over that day and can use the day in any fashion He thinks appropriate. Consequently, the disciples were not breaking the law; they were simply feeding themselves as they were walking about learning from Jesus, the God of the day of rest.

What will you do on your Sabbath day? Rest in the knowledge that Jesus ordained that day for you! So, spend it with Him and learn how to love like the Serving King…

JP

DAY 129

The Value of People

"To be doing good deeds is man's most glorious task." —Sophocles

Going on from that place, He went into their synagogue, and a man with a shriveled hand was there. Looking for a reason to bring charges against Jesus, they asked Him, "Is it lawful to heal on the Sabbath?" He said to them, "If any of you has a sheep and it falls into a pit on the Sabbath, will you not take hold of it and lift it out? How much more valuable is a person than a sheep! Therefore it is lawful to do good on the Sabbath." (Matthew 12:9-12)

The religious leaders must have thought they knew Jesus' answer to their question. But, as was His custom, He responded by asking a question that would not only relay His answer but would indict those inquiring. The fact Jesus could heal had become a foregone conclusion. Yet, the religious leaders, always looking for a way to implicate Jesus, would tempt Him to break the Sabbath by doing a miracle. Jesus knew their ploy, and He knew the law had been altered to allow for animals to be retrieved from a pit on the Sabbath, because they were so important to the economic health of the community.

But what about a person who was not important to the economic life of the community? What if they were a drain on society? In those days, a crippled man would have had a difficult, if not impossible, time finding work, thus, a beggar. The value society and religious leaders put on such a person would not even come close to the value they had for their livestock. Yet, Jesus made a profound statement in comparing the value of an animal to a person, especially, a crippled man. The comparison alone would have been considered going against the law. They may have argued the man's life was not in danger, yet a sheep having fallen into a pit could have been. What harm would come waiting one more day to heal the man?

This event gives us insight into how precious human life is to God no matter the perceived economic or societal value. A person has value in the eyes of the Lord, because people are the only creatures on earth made in His image. All people, regardless of intelligence, wealth, health, age, political party, or sin are made in the image of God and will always have greater value than any other creation. It is always the best idea to do good to another human being, regardless of the mantra of the day! Love on like the Serving King...

MR

Stealing Healing

"Nothing is so healing as the human touch." —Bobby Fischer

Then He said to the man, "Stretch out your hand." So he stretched it out and it was completely restored, just as sound as the other. But the Pharisees went out and plotted how they might kill Jesus. (Matthew 12:13-14)

As bold as the conversation was leading up to now, it is not surprising Jesus healed the man with the shriveled hand completely! He now had two useful hands! This man experienced an incredible gift of mercy changing his life forever, and for which Jesus asked nothing in return. Still, the Pharisees were committed to determine how they could kill Him.

Modern Pharisees still plague in the western world. I have seen many times when Jesus shows up and a miracle or His presence is experienced, and someone attempts to kill and nullify what happened. They claim that person cannot really be changed; let's just wait and see. Or, that marriage won't last, she can't really forgive him for what he did. Are you sure his cancer was healed by God? Why didn't God heal my husband? These and many other challenges are leveled against Jesus and our experience.

It is at that time we must recall that our battle is not against flesh and blood, but against rulers of darkness in this age. The enemy fights back when he sees a life saved, a family re-united, someone healed from cancer, or a shriveled-up hand restored. He fights because he is scared! He is scared of the same thing the Pharisees were scared of; Jesus' ability to attract followers that are wholly devoted and committed to Him. Remember when Jesus was tempted by the devil in the desert? Every time Satan tempted Jesus, his purpose was to steal, kill, or destroy the plan the Father had for Him and ultimately for us. His tactics don't really change much, but we are not unaware of his schemes. Don't cave into the fear mongering and the sly tactics the enemy will throw at you. You are made in the image of God, uniquely designed to love like the Serving King...
MR

Justice Of Another Kind

"Reconciliation should be accompanied by justice, otherwise it will not last. While we all hope for peace it shouldn't be peace at any cost, but peace based on principle, on justice." —Corazon Aquino

Behold, My Servant whom I have chosen, My Beloved with Whom My soul is will pleased. I will put My Spirit upon Him, and He will proclaim justice to the Gentiles. (Matthew 12:18)

The story is often told of the little boy on Easter morning, sitting next to his mother, quietly whispering in her ear, "I love Jesus, but His father really makes me mad!" God the Father, the wrath slinger, often gets a bad rap for His antics surrounding the cross of the Serving King. The novice rarely "rejoices in God" in the early experiences of the cross.

But reconciliation is a comprehensive act, concerned with so much more than just melting the hardened heart of the enemies of God as they behold the cross, critical as that may be. Hence, the cross of Jesus proclaims reconciliation as horribly expensive, much more than mere forgiveness, displaying justice as the foundation of peace. But even the novice, bewildered and confused at the foot of the cross, knows this is no ordinary justice, the guilty paying for their transgressions. This is profoundly different, a different justice in which the guilty, now desperate to pay their own way as they agonize over the gravity of the Son's punishment, can only watch as the wrath of God reigns down on the Son, the Son who begged for another way (Luke 22:42-44).

It is the justice of vicarious suffering through substitutionary atonement, a horrible experience in which the guilty agonize as the innocent one pays the bill for the guilty. No one gets away scot-free, justice simply does not work that way. The guilty, finally understanding the transaction between Father and Son, shudder at His feet, unable to bear the agony of the innocent in their stead. And then, a final moment of comprehension, the agony of the Father as the reign of justice unfolds upon the Son. And so, "we also rejoice in God," willing to suffer with the Son for the sake of the enemies of God. Loving like the Serving King leads many to their cross. Love on with courage…
DM

Victory

"The profound thing in man is his will, not sin. Will is the essential element in God's creation of man: sin is a perverse disposition which entered into man."
—*Oswald Chambers*

He will not quarrel or cry aloud, nor will anyone hear His voice in the streets; a bruised reed He will not break, and a smoldering wick He will not quench, until He brings justice to victory; and His name the Gentiles will hope.

(Matthew 12:19-21)

You began your trek after the Serving King under great duress. Such is the simple reality for all trekkers, crippled by a will enslaved to sin. Yet, the will remembers what it was designed to do in trekking after the Serving King and so begins the battle for mastery of the will. Sin is no easy opponent, fighting for mastery of the will in each moment, finding victory in far too many battles along the way. Although, many, liberated by the prevenient empowering grace of God, choose to 'trek after' the Serving King.

Immediately upon taking the first step of this great trek, God continued a 'good work' in you, a restoration of the will liberating from sin, the will's old taskmaster, and freeing it to 'do' what the will was always meant to do: please God. Once engaged on the trek after God, God responds toward the will, "...for it is God who works in you, both to will and to work for His good pleasure" (Philippians 2:13). As you quickly discover, God does not intend to work alone. No, God has liberated the will to work with God, alongside God, in this 'restoration' of not only will, but, additionally, the life of the one who has been redeemed.

However, this 'work out' requires great effort on the part of the 'liberated will' and it must engage a flesh that has been infected in the most profound manner by sin, that nagging inhibitor, the great detractor of all movements toward the 'divine'. Therein lies the great first effort for the liberated will, the subduction of the flesh, returning it toward its original calling: pleasing God. Be not surprised as a persistent 'fear and trembling' lingers in your being. You have engaged in this battle many times before and lost, as the flesh, infected and empowered by sin, reigned over your will, rendering you a slave to its desires. But things have changed in the most profound manner, for God is now at work within you, empowering the will in ways never before imagined. The victory is now yours. All that remains is to simply work it out in the midst of hope. Those who love in the way of the Serving King will hope in the power of love...

DM

DAY 133

Blasphemy!

"A house divided against itself cannot stand." —Abraham Lincoln

Then a demon-oppressed man who was blind and mute was brought to Him and He healed him, so that the man spoke and saw. And all the people were amazed, and said "can this be the Son of David?" But when the Pharisees heard it, they said "It is only by Beelzebub, the prince of demons, that this man casts out demons." (Matthew 12:22-27)

I occasionally enjoy magic shows. I understand that it is magic, that I am being manipulated to believe something that is not real. But never actually am I fooled to think that someone can do authentic magic. I can tell the difference between magic tricks and miracles.

It was common in the ancient world for exorcists to try and manipulate the spiritual world. They had many tricks and could do many wonders. They often tried to make people believe that what they did was truth, that they had special powers. And sometimes they believed it themselves! But people often understood that their magic was somehow unreal. But when Jesus commanded demons, it was from His own place of authority, and when the demons immediately submitted, this was different. This was a miracle. This required power from a different source. The crowd understood this, asking if He could be the anticipated Son of David. Obviously, this did not go over well with the Pharisees. They wanted to discredit Jesus and retain their own power.

The Pharisees accused Jesus of using Satan's power and practicing magic, a crime punishable by death by stoning. But this time, Jesus defended Himself. His logic was impeccable. How can a kingdom stand if it is divided against itself? Even the Pharisees could not refute this. The Pharisees were known to often exorcise demons, putting into question their motivation. Jesus asked them to come clean, to disclose the evil intentions within their hearts. By whom do your sons cast out demons? Saying their own sons would be their judges. To deny Jesus' power would cast their own actions into judgement. They accuse Jesus of blasphemy, but their own actions are instead blasphemy of the top order, to accuse Jesus of being an agent of Satan! The Pharisees were becoming desperate. The people saw that Jesus was performing miracles, and they were still trying to discredit Him and make Him somehow a fraud. This only reflected on their evil intentions. But understand, once unleashed, the love of the Serving King is simply too powerful to harness. Love on in the way of the Serving King...

PG

Irrefutable Logic

"The strong man is the one who is able to intercept at will the communication between the senses and the mind." —Napoleon Bonaparte

But if it is by the Spirit of God that I cast out demons, then the Kingdom of God has come upon you. Or how can someone enter a strong man's house and plunder his goods, unless he first binds the strong man? Then indeed he may plunder his house. Whoever is not with Me is against Me, and whoever does not gather with Me scatters." (Matthew 12:28-30)

The blinders have been taken off. The logic is undeniable. The evidence is mounting. Only fools can deny what Jesus is saying now. He cannot be any clearer.

Jesus continued to defend His Kingdom to the Pharisees. Obviously, a kingdom fighting against itself cannot stand. The accusation of using Satan's power to defeat Satan was illogical. And it was blasphemy against the Holy Spirit indeed. The hole the accusers were digging was getting very deep. That which they were accusing Him becomes the evil that they themselves are charged with.

Jesus now speaks very plainly. He openly declares that His Kingdom, God's Kingdom, had come. He was done making subtle references and using metaphors. He knew His time was short. He was declaring to the crowds that He was who He was, who they suspected Him of being. He provided irrefutably strong evidence that God was the power behind His miracles and teachings. The implied connection to all people waiting on their Messiah, of the strong man being bound, was that of the Messiah binding Satan during the Messianic age, a known image. The Messiah was to return Israel to its glory and gather up all the spoils. He declared that He was that Messiah. And not only that, He was authorized to judge the world. And would. Not the Pharisees, not the other religious leaders, but Jesus.

Jesus challenged His listeners, stating that there was no room for neutrality much less opposition! For if you were not for Him, you were against Him. Indifference or apathy is characterized as opposition and is against Him. He asks for people to be completely committed to Him and to the Kingdom of God. He clarifies further that gathering souls for the Kingdom of God is the work, and those who did not gather would be scattered as chaff scatters in the wind. A healthy harvest is needed, and workers are essential to the task. Jesus calls us to love aggressively as we chase on after the Serving King....

PG

DAY 135

An Unwanted Pardon

"We are all full of weakness and errors; let us mutually pardon each other our follies - it is the first law of nature." —Voltaire

Therefore, I tell you, every sin and blasphemy will be forgiven people, but the blasphemy against the Spirit will not be forgiven. And whoever speaks a word against the Son of Man will be forgiven, but whoever speaks against the Holy Spirit will not be forgiven, either in this age or in the age to come.

(Matthew 12:31-32)

Ever have that moment of concern, "Have I committed the unpardonable sin at some time in my life?" How do we know if we have? First, let me say, blasphemy of the Holy Spirit is not an act of ignorance, or unintelligent abstention from what Christ has done in this world. The Pharisees were witnesses of what Jesus was doing while He walked the earth and attributed His works to Beelzebub instead of God. This was unforgivable because they did not recognize the only one who could forgive them as Messiah, thus rejecting the Holy Spirit drawing them to repentance.

To die unpardonably is to continue a life of unbelief, finally dying in a state of belief. The Holy Spirit draws us, if we reject His drawing conviction and chose to remain unrepentant, in the truest since of the term we have chosen hell over Heaven. It's unpardonable to die without faith in Christ. God's Word clearly tells all who listen (John 3:16-18), "For God so loved the world, that He gave His only Son, that whoever believes in Him should not perish but have eternal life. For God did not send His Son into the world to condemn the world, but in order that the world might be saved through Him. Whoever believes in Him is not condemned, but whoever does not believe is condemned already, because he has not believed in the name of the only Son of God."

Many people fear they have committed some sin that God cannot or will not forgive, and there is no hope for them, no matter what they do. Satan would like nothing more than to keep people bound under that misconception. Yet, God gives encouragement to the sinner who is convicted of his sin: "Come near to God and He will come near to you" (James 4:8). The Holy Spirit is always drawing, 'come near' and do not reject, and you will be saved. Embrace the love of the Serving King…
TM

What Kind Of Tree

"The right thing to do with habits is to lose them in the life of the Lord, until every habit is so practiced that there is no conscious habit at all. Our spiritual life continually resolves into introspection because there are some qualities we have not added as yet." —Oswald Chambers

"Either make the tree good and its fruit good, or the tree bad and its fruit bad, for the tree is known by its fruit." (Matthew 12:33)

At some point in this trek after the Serving King, you will begin to realize the trek ought to be more than simply a long walk with the King. You will pause to ask, "Is there any fruit from this journey I am on? Is this walk productive for me or for others?" In that moment, you will have hit a key mark in your transformation into a 'Christ Follower' in which pragmatism matters.

Yet, some trekkers will be content in their knowledge of our Lord Jesus Christ, but for those who trek closely with the King, there will be no satisfaction in the luxurious life of head knowledge left unapplied, for, by definition, 'unapplied knowledge' is ineffective and unfruitful. Instead, these few trekkers will radically examine the 'productivity' of their efforts and, upon finding shortcomings creating a fruitless life, will continually engage in introspection, looking for "some qualities we have not added yet," some virtues that are yet missing, some way of being that is still absent from day-to-day living. Thus, comes the need to ensure these qualities are increasingly yours.

Beware, introspection is fraught with pitfalls for those trekking after the Serving King. Introspection reveals a good number of virtues, these qualities still needing to be added to your repertoire, and it can be overwhelming, unless the trekker remembers God is the source of all 'virtues' yet lacking in the being of the trekker. Your responsibility is simply to make every effort (2 Peter 1:5). It is God who provides the missing virtues, as God endues your 'every effort' with a power beyond what you are able to provide. "For it is God who works in you, both to will and to work for His good pleasure" (Philippians 2:13). Yours is simply to make every effort as you trek on. Every effort is the fertilizer empowering the life of those determined to love in the way of the Serving King...
DM

Do Over

"Every man dies. Not every man really lives." —William Wallace

I tell you, on the day of judgment people will give account for every careless word they speak, for by your words you will be justified, and by your words you will be condemned. (Matthew 12:36)

The many delight in blaming that one man, Adam, for the utter chaos and foolishness of sin running rampant in the human condition, and rightly so, given inherited depravity. And oh, the delight in freedom from responsibility because of the sin of that one man enslaving the many (all) into the infection of sin. But sin, comprehensive and invasive as it may be, is never the last word concerning the human condition. The Serving King provides a grand do over for those wise enough to embrace His offer.

In the one act of righteousness, the cross of Jesus Christ, the grand do over is loosed upon all people, nullifying inherited condemnation and loss of life, infusing justification and life upon, and in, all people. And with life, the restoration of a radically altered and diminished Adamic freewill comes that which the many, perhaps all, dread more than any evil, personal responsibility and accountability before God.

But the grand do over is rarely embraced by the many, refusing to receive the abundance of grace, instead wallowing in the depravity of Adam, thinking themselves released from the trauma of personal responsibility and accountability before God. But like death, invasive and non-discriminating, life invades all men (people), relentless in its determination to infuse justification and life unto all people, the universal do over. And with life comes the opportunity and responsibility to receive the abundance of grace made available to all men (Romans 5:17).

Tragically, the grand do over ends poorly for those refusing to really live. Long enslaved to old ways of being and doing, the freed man returns to the slave master of old, surrendering life to whims of the old master. The grand tragedy of life appears as life slips away yet again, and this time Adam is nowhere to be found. Dare to step into the love offered by the Serving King...
DM

Seek His Face...

"If you seek God's hand, you will miss His face. If you seek His face, you will get His hand also." —Daniel Henderson

"Some Scribes and Pharisees said to Him, Teacher, we want to see a sign from You. And He said to them, "An evil and adulterous generation craves for a sign." (Matthew 12:38)

Craving a 'sign' came with an intense rebuke in Matthew 12:38. Is receiving and craving a sign two different things? Or is one a result of another? Let's look at some of the patriarchs of the faith and see how God revealed Himself to them as they sought Him.

Abraham was told by God that he would be a father of many. "Abraham believed God, and God credited to him as righteousness" (Gen 15:6, Gal 3:6). Abraham never saw the magnitude of God's promise, but Abraham followed God in Faith, walking in His ways and obeying His lead. Seeking His face does not mean we will always see signs or results immediately. Moses served and followed God into the Promised Land with the Israelites; what a task.

But Moses would not go unless the Lord went before Him. Moses was rather persistent in telling God, I won't go unless You go before me. In Exodus 33:12-23, God allowed him to see His glory pass by him in the cleft of the rock; but he saw His back not His face. With a half a million people following Moses, he needed to know that God was leading him. God honored His request, as Moses needed to know it was God's leading and not his own.

Seeking His face is worshipping and seeking His character, trusting His Word, and obeying what He tells us. When we do that, miracles do happen and situations fall into a divine order. Matt 6:33 says, when we "seek FIRST the Kingdom of God and all His righteousness, then all these things will be added to you." Signs will follow those who believe, who step out in faith to do the things God's Word says.

When you follow Christ and there is a need for a sign (a healing or a provision), God will move. Don't put the horse before the cart. Seeking a sign first to demonstrate God's character is not faith in His ways or character, it's unbelief. But when we seek the Serving King's face, we will be blessed to see His hand move! Seek the face of the serving King, and all these things will be added to you! Love on in the ways of the Serving King...
SB

DAY 139

SIGNs

"Sign, Sign everywhere a sign. Blockin' out the scenery. Breakin' my mind, Do this, don't do that. Can't you read the sign?" – Five Man Electrical Band

"And yet no sign will be given to (this adulterous generation), except the sign of Jonah the prophet, for just as Jonah was three day and three nights in the belly of a sea monster, so will the Son of Man be three days and three nights in the heart of the earth." (Matt 12:39-40)

Signs are everywhere! The Five Man Electrical Band in 1970 wrote a song in rebellion to all the signs telling us what we have to do. In our culture today, many do not want to be told what to do, they want to be their own boss. And when it comes to God, they want Him to give them signs in order to believe, or have faith that He is really exists.

Virtues of the faith seem to be slowly vanishing, like trust and teachability. We would rather demand to do it our way and seek our own understanding for the truth. I admit, I have to repent of following my own ways daily.

The scribes and Pharisees wanted Jesus to prove His divinity, instead He humbled Himself to the point of death, even death on a cross. Jesus' Kingdom was not of this world, and when He resurrected, they still didn't believe. So what sign would have made a difference? The reference of Jonah and the whale didn't make a lasting difference, so what other sign could Jesus have done to demonstrate His love for us?

The end of the song by the Five Man Electrical Band had an interesting verse. "And the sign said, Everybody welcome. Come in kneel down and pray, but when they passed around the plate at the end of it all, I didn't have a penny to pay. So I got me a pen and a paper and I made up my own little sign, I said, "Thank you Lord, for thinkin' about me. I'm alive and doing fine.""

This verse, even in rebellion to signs, had a point to make, that God loves them, which is true. But being alive and doing fine, did they really know Him? Are you living by faith or needing a sign as you follow the Serving King today? Those who love Him rarely need a sign as they chase on...

SB

DAY 140

Something is Missing

"As Luke 24 shows, it's possible to read the Bible, study the Bible, and memorize large portions of the Bible, while missing the whole point of the Bible."
—*Tullian Tchividjian*

"When the unclean spirit has gone out of a person, it passes through waterless places seeking rest, but finds none. Then it says, 'I will return to my house from which I came.' And when it comes, it finds the house empty, swept, and put in order. Then it goes and brings with it seven other spirits more evil than itself...
(Matthew 12:43-45)

Demons, fallen angels, evil spirits, etc., call them what you will; however, no matter their name, one thing remains unescapable . . . they are real. One of the greatest lies Satan has convinced humans to adopt as truth is that he himself does not actually exist and neither do his minions. Jesus encountered demons throughout His ministry, casting them out of people on several occasions. If ever there was someone who could be considered an expert on the behaviors and practices of demons, it is Jesus.

Jesus tells us a story of a demon leaving a person, but after uncomfortably wandering around, the demon grabs several of his buddies and they all go and repossess that same person. The problem was seemingly taken care of and everything set to right. However, now the person's problem was several times worse. This passage unavoidably begs certain questions. How can a demon that is cast out in Jesus' name go back and repossess a believer? Is Jesus not strong enough to protect those who are His? Let the questions linger for a moment and dive deeper into the passage. The problem is not a lack of power on Jesus' part, but a lack of presence of Jesus – having not been invited into the heart of the person now freed from a demon's control. The demon goes back and finds the house empty. Miracles are wonderful gifts from God, but most are temporary gifts from a loving Father. The miracle that eclipses all others is the miracle of the active and intimate presence of Jesus in our daily lives and the gift of the Holy Spirit to heal, lead, and correct us.

Jesus' statements in this passage are not meant to be a "how to" on exorcisms as much as a rebuke to the generation of people around Him. The people around Him looked spiritually healthy but were, in reality, as bad off as the possessed person. They were missing the key ingredient to a healthy spiritual life . . . Jesus. As we go through this day, may we actually engage with Jesus and allow Him to shine through us as we love on in the ways of the Serving King...
MS

DAY 141

Unexpected Brothers and Sisters...

"The only way you're going to reach places you've never gone is if you trust God's direction to do things you've never done." —Germany Kent

"Here are my mother and my brothers! For whoever does the will of My Father in Heaven is My brother and sister and mother." (Matthew 12:46-50)

Do you know anyone who has trouble sitting still? Maybe this description fits you. There are people who have to be doing something all of the time. These people like to work and really struggle when there is nothing to do. Sometimes, Christianity is a struggle for these types of people. There are those times when we are told the value of reading the Bible or spending certain periods of time in prayer or meditation. There have even been those who have suggested that people who do not spend a certain amount of time in these solitary pursuits are not the vibrant Christian they could be.

This is unfortunate. It is at this point that some might accuse me of being against prayer, but that is not true. A deep, contemplative prayer life is a wonderful gift to have and discipline to practice. It would be a great thing if more people pursued this path. However, not everyone finds it easy, or even desirable to pursue this life. There are people who find extended times of quiet to be quite the hurdle. For these people, our Biblical passage should be quite affirming. Thankfully, for many of us, those who do the will of God are considered God's family. I like how this identity is described with a verb of action. I think it is true that the world needs more people of prayer. I also think it is undeniably true that we do not have near enough people who do God's will. Prayer is a good thing, meditation is a good thing, but, at some point, someone has to do the thing that is needed. Maybe you are one of the people who like to be doing things. If you are, do them for the glory of God.

It is one thing to make that statement, but quite another to live it. How does one live this type of life? First, love God with all your heart, soul, mind, and strength, and then do what you want. The point is that loving God with our whole being changes what we desire to do. The second bit of advice would be this – in all of doing, we must remain open to the leading of the Spirit. To people of action, this might be a great prayer. "God, this seems like the right path for me, so I will pursue it with all I am. However, You can stop or re-direct me at any time. I seek Your will." Our world needs both types of people. While one group is praying like never before, may a group of doers be unleashed as well. Both are critical aspects of loving like the Serving King...
DW

DAY 142

Successful Sowing

"Our greatest fear should not be of failure but of succeeding at things in life that don't really matter." —Francis Chan

"A farmer went out to sow his seed. As he was scattering the seed, some fell along the path, and the birds came and ate it up. Some fell on rocky places, where it did not have much soil. It sprang up quickly, because the soil was shallow. 6 But when the sun came up, the plants were scorched, and they withered because they had no root. Other seed fell among thorns, which grew up and choked the plants." (Matthew 13:3-7)

It is the responsibility of those who follow Christ to share the love and truth with others who do not know Him. Imagine the privilege of being invited to be a tool in the salvation of a human being. However, in the United States, we are currently closing more churches than we open every year. Numbers of those who attend worship services are dropping. The question is why?

The answer for many lies in the word 'fear'. One of the greatest fears plaguing the church today is the fear of failure. When people are worried about failing, they begin to question whether it is worth trying. It can freeze people in their tracks and keep them from accomplishing anything at all. This said fact leads to less people coming to know Jesus as Lord.

What we have to remember is that we are charged with sowing the seed. There will, no doubt, be obstacles and trials along the way. Some seed will not take root, but other seeds will. Despite the obstacles and spiritual warfare that goes on all around us, some seed will sprout.

Remember that there is something that you can do. You can work the soil, preparing it for the seed. Pray for those whom you will come into contact. Build real personal relationships with those who you are ministering. Care about them and be part of their lives. Help them to see the trials that go on around them and be there when you can. Presence is a powerful tool as we love in the way of the Serving King…
ME

Multiplication

"If God is your partner, make your plans BIG!" —D.L. Moody

"Still other seed fell on good soil, where it produced a crop—a hundred, sixty or thirty times what was sown. Whoever has ears, let them hear."(Matthew 13:8-9)

There was once a man who had always dreamed of being farmer. Every time he drove past fields, it lifted his spirit. He was mesmerized by the new life. The crops dancing in the breeze made his heart sing. The smell in the air put a smile on his face. It was a calling for him. Something that he just couldn't get away from.

Upon reaching a certain age, he decided to purchase a local farm that was for sale. He was finally going to fulfill his calling. So, he purchased some seed and equipment and went about planting his first field. At the end of the day, he looked out over his work and was very pleased. He climbed into bed and couldn't wait to see the results of this day of hard work.

As the sun rose into the sky, he jumped out of bed and ran to the field to see what had happened. Only, nothing could actually be seen. He put his head in his hands in frustration. He realized that accomplishing this calling was going to take much more work than he had imagined. He had to make a decision. Would he continue working to see it through or walk away?

The same is true when we plant seeds for the Kingdom of God. It is not as simple as many think. It can take a lifetime of love and work to nurture the seeds that are planted. In fact, sometimes one person plants the seed; while another actually will see the seed flourish.

When we go forth to share the Good News, it is not a one day or one-time thing. Seeds need the right conditions and the right nutrients to develop and to grow strong. The people that we reach with the message of the Good News need the same. They need time and the proper nutrients. They need to know that they are not a project to you, but people who God truly loves through you. They need to see life modeled before them and have people to guide and show them the way. May God work through you to multiply the seed of the Kingdom of God as you love on in the ways of the Serving King...
ME

Why?

Thinking is the hardest work there is, which is probably the reason why so few engage in it.—Henry Ford

Then the disciples came and asked Him, "Why do you speak to them in parables?" He answered... (Matthew 13:10)

In our quest after the Serving King, we continually encounter the unforeseen. Try as we might, we do not yet understand Jesus. Like the disciples, once in awhile we cannot help ourselves and ask Him, "Why?" Then He answers, stunning us with a response so unexpected we are rendered speechless.

The unexpectedness is not in what He says, rather in that He answers us at all. This is an emblem of the sort of relationship He truly offers us. We struggle imagining a king stooping to meet a lowly subject, engaging in a conversation with one that has failed the king repeatedly. How much more so when we question the king's behavior? But Jesus, the Serving King, is also the Great Teacher, the One challenging us to go deeper and deeper still.

Those still awed by the offer of any relationship with God find themselves struggling to keep up in the quest. Intimidated by the prospect of being in the presence of the King, they are too ashamed to be intimate and let their defenses down. It is all too much to believe that God would spend any time explaining Himself to me. The intimidated denies God the right to value him, instead deeming himself unworthy, he falls behind.

But those humble enough to dismiss any personal sense of worth – or worthlessness – hunts after the ways of the King in earnest. Freed from the pretense of place, taking Jesus at His word, we recklessly ask Him about His ways. Having left ego behind long ago, the fear of an undignified question does not cross the mind, as we relentlessly pursue our insatiable desire to know the Serving King a little more. Before processing the possible interpretations of our inquiry, we blurt out "Why?" Like a child, we are completely without guise. And, recognizing our sincerity, He answers us. He knows we cannot Love like a Servant if we do not know the Servant. He delights in preparing us to be like Him. Ask away and keep loving...

BS

Keep Thinking

There are no secrets that time does not reveal. —Jean Racine

"To you it has been given to know the secrets of the Kingdom of Heaven, but to them it has not been given. For to those who have, more will be given, and they will have an abundance; but from those who have nothing, even what they have will be taken away. The reason I speak to them in parables is that 'seeing they do not perceive, and hearing they do not listen, nor do they understand.'"

(Matthew 13:11-13)

The immature hear these words and scoff, unable to reconcile the loving, compassionate ways of the Serving King with a message of exclusion. We wonder how it is that Jesus would deny His people the opportunity to understand His message, to attempt adopting His ways. Is not everyone worthy of the Gospel? What is the point of being obtuse and difficult? It is at this point, a seemingly harsh answer irreconcilable with the Man we thought we knew, that we wonder if we have the will to go further. Maybe we will rest here until He gives a better explanation.

Those willing to do the hard work, to follow Jesus wherever He would go, do not rest here long. The willing mull over in their hearts and minds the response given by the Serving King. They ask, "Could it be I am missing something?" As they contemplate His words, deeper meanings are considered. And then comes the a-ha moment – it is this very act, the spiritual contemplative reflection that unlocks the mysteries of God. The yearning of the heart expands the mind to receive what the Holy Spirit wants so desperately to provide. Following Jesus is futile for those who resist giving up old ways of thinking. The new heart necessitates a transforming of the mind. The mind cannot receive something new without releasing something old.

This leads to recognition that God is not denying His mercy and grace to those seeking it. On the contrary, the Serving King is being gracious and merciful in His methods. Ever the wise Shepherd, He is leading those that recognize His voice. Those who desire a new message, a new way of being and doing, are caused to open their hearts and minds through prayerful reflection. Those that have resisted a dulling of the heart are granted the privilege of learning to love like the Serving King. Keep loving as you ponder…
BS

Closed

"People only see what they are prepared to see." —*Ralph Waldo Emerson*

With them indeed is fulfilled the prophecy of Isaiah that says: 'You will indeed listen, but never understand, and you will indeed look... But blessed are your eyes, for they see, and your ears, for they hear. Truly I tell you, many prophets and righteous people longed to see what you see, but did not see it, and to hear what you hear, but did not hear it." (Matthew 13:14-17)

There are those that will 'never understand,' 'never perceive,' and not receive the healing of the Great Physician. These meet Jesus with a hardened heart and closed mind. Some are tempted to judge these, assuming their hardened heart is some overt rejection of God. The Serving King gazes pitifully upon them as they neglect the offer that so many others see for the treasure it is. He senses with sorrow that most of these have been so twisted by the world they cannot conceive the unconventional wisdom inherent in His radical way of being and doing. Driven by compassion, His urgency increases all the more.

Then there are 'the prophets and the righteous,' people whose fate it was to predate the Messiah. These are held up as examples of true faith, those that endured without the opportunity to 'see what you see,' and 'hear what you hear.' Despite the as-yet unfulfilled promise of the coming King, they held firm to their tender hearts and open minds, awaiting the day God would intervene and change everything. It is these that bring us to our knees in gratitude. How fortunate are we to experience the mercies of the Serving King firsthand! Our faith need not be tested in the silence as was that of 'the prophets and the righteous.'

So, we are blessed to be able to open our eyes and listen with our ears. We may just catch a glimpse of God's true nature if we look closely enough. Listening hard enough we can hear the Serving King chuckle as He tells another 'you have heard it said...but I tell you...,' explaining yet again what elusively slips through our grasp, the principles of the Kingdom of God. Those yearning to catch Him are ever finding ways to mute the noise and still the picture, straining to see and hear. Pay close attention, listening carefully, and keep loving...
BS

Stolid Heart

To see things in the seed, that is genius." —Lau Tzo

"Hear then the parable of the sower: When anyone hears the word of the kingdom and does not understand it, the evil one comes and snatches away what has been sown in his heart. This is what was sown along the path."

(Matthew 13:18-19)

Jane Austen's classic novel, Sense & Sensibility, tells the tale of two sisters: Elinor, who is wise, and Marianne, who is emotional. Together, they are "sense (wise) and sensibility (emotional)". Although this team of two works together to create a powerful duo, each only brought one main element to the table.

The Parable of the Sower shows that the sower is the same, the seed is consistent, and the soil can vary. The seed is the Word of God, and the soil is the heart of one listening. So, we look at the first seed thrown onto the wayward path. This heart hears the Word of the Lord but does not know experientially the truth that is being spoken. In Ancient Greek, to "listen" would mean to "hear and obey." If hearing is of the Word, which brings truth, then obedience occurs when the heart is moved into action, repentance, and a desire for understanding. We cannot separate the two and expect growth.

In John 4:23, Jesus explains to the woman at the well that true worshippers "worship the Father both in Spirit and in Truth." These two cannot be separated. One cannot only bring truth and wisdom and rely on someone else to bring spirit, emotion, and sensibility, therefore creating one "true worshipper." We must all worship in sense and sensibility, truth and love.

This soil cannot generate growth, because their heart has been hardened. Maybe it is calloused from consistent hardships of this world, previous experience with religion, or because of deep pain inflicted by someone they once loved. No matter the reason, the seed was thrown upon the soil but not in the soil. Because it sat there in full exposure, the enemy quickly comes and snatches the seed like a seagull on the beach when bread is left on the sand. If we find our hearts hardened, hearing truth but not taking it to heart, let us pray for the Spirit to breathe life into our spirits, learning to accept the abounding love and grace of the Serving King who gives to all who worship Him in spirit and in truth. Love on in the ways of the Serving King…

AG

DAY 148

Shallow Heart

"It's easy to be a short-term hero." —Paul Polman

"As for what was sown on rocky ground, this is the one who hears the word and immediately receives it with joy, yet he has no root in himself, but endures for a while, and when tribulation or persecution arises on account of the word, immediately he falls away." (Matthew 13:20-21)

James tells us this in his writing to take joy in the midst of tribulation, because it is in that moment that we will grow (1:2-4). There is joy to be found in the midst of the trials we endure. As believers, because of the truth of God's Word, we are able to stand firm during times of drought, extreme heat, and tribulations of all kinds.

But today, we look at the seed that falls on rocky soil. At first, the Word is received with astounding joy because of the promise of hope, grace, love, and peace. The heart is set on fire, readily stirred with emotion. Although the excitement of the promises of these fruits lasts awhile, the root is non-existent. Trials come. Persecution arises. This seed found in the rocks cannot handle denial, tribulations, and the realization that sometimes emotions come to an end, and it withers away in the heat.

Sometimes, all we have left is the truth on which we stand. But in this case, there are no roots, no truth. As we discussed yesterday, we are to worship in Spirit and Truth. During the weight of persecution, worshipping in Spirit has withered, and there is no truth on which to cling for those who have a shallow understanding of the Word. The top layer of soil seemed promising, but the rocks eventually got in the way. Jesus becomes the stumbling block. The truth of the Word has caused them fall away.

As the drought comes, trials occur, and tribulations take over, remember that God has promised to never leave you or forsake you. Jesus says He is with us always, even until the end (Matthew 28:20). When the emotions are fading and God's presence seems distant, hold tightly to the truth that is the anchor in the midst of the storm. Believe that the Spirit will continue to move, and the truth will begin to take root. It is then when growth will occur and God the Father will be truly worshipped through hearing and understanding the word. Love on in the ways of the Serving King...
AG

DAY 149

Every Rose Has Its Thorn?

"But he that dares not grasp the thorn Should never crave the rose."
—Anne Bronte

"As for what was sown among thorns, this is the one who hears the word, but the cares of the world and the deceitfulness of riches choke the word, and it proves unfruitful." (Matthew 13:22)

"No one can serve two masters," Jesus tells His followers earlier in Matthew 6:24. There will come a point in each person's life when they will have to choose which one they will follow: God or money.

Most believers have every intention of being fruitful. Upon hearing the Word, they have learned the truth in the mind and understanding in the heart. The seed sown among the thorns does not seem to be in immediate trouble. The soil appears to be fertile soil, and, in fact, there might even be a blade now sprouting forth above the surface. What we cannot see is the seed of thorns and thistles sleeping dormant underground next to the seeds of the Word.

With some time, the good and bad seeds begin to grow simultaneously, competing for space, sap, and sunshine. The seeds of thorns start to strangle the roots of the fruit. Eventually, the thorns are towering over the grain in both height and breadth. This lack of sunshine will cause a lack of fruit-bearing.

The world's ways can become more enticing, distracting, and weighing, because thorns and thistles we have chosen to leave in our hearts are strangling the light of the Spirit and Truth in us. No matter the good intentions and principles set in places, if the bad is left in with the good, the journey of sanctification will be a difficult road; So much so, that the heart will become choked out of the hope it once had, bearing no fruit from the once-promising seed.

In our journey, not only are we supposed to be obedient in the things we ought to do but also in that which we ought not to do. As we grow in our walk with Christ, there will be "seeds" that you must get rid of in order to grow deeper roots and to bear fruit. What are the worries, distractions, or cares of this world hindering your growth as you chase after the Serving King? Fear not and love on in the ways of the Serving King...
AG

The Steady Heart

"It's the steady, quiet, plodding ones who win in the lifelong race."
—*Robert W. Service*

"As for what was sown on good soil, this is the one who hears the word and understands it. He indeed bears fruit and yields, in one case a hundredfold, in another sixty, and in another thirty." (Matthew 13:23)

Walking the land of Palestine today would not appear much different when it comes to the farming techniques used in the days Jesus walked the Earth. You would see farmers with a bag of seed thrown over their shoulder, walking the rows of the harvest field, tossing handfuls of seeds to the ground before returning to plow the rows.

Tenfold would be considered a good crop to the crowd of followers to which Jesus was speaking. And yet, Jesus explains that the harvest of the good soil would yield hundredfold, sixty, and thirty! Imagine what they must have been thinking! How can it be that a seed so small could produce such an abundant, and almost incomprehensible, return?

Fruit is the outcome of a heart that has received the Word of the Lord and has not only heard what it says in their mind but believes and understands with their heart. Obedience, no matter the cost, results in a great harvest. Consistency of actions and an absence of hurry are required. Patience is key to understanding that there is a time for reaping and a time for harvest. The reaping is the diligent, faithful process of working in the fields, even when you want to quit. The harvest is the exciting season of abundance and growth that makes the season of reaping worth it!

And when the harvest comes, there is proof in the fruit it produces. Galatians 5:22-23 lists the fruit of the Spirit: love, joy, peace, patience, kindness, goodness, faithfulness, gentleness, and self-control. These are the evidences of the Spirit working in your heart and in your life. The more we know the truth and understand with our heart, we begin to obey in each aspect of our lives. It may take time - well, if we are doing this "right," it will take time. So take heart, keep being obedient, gaining wisdom, and asking for understanding. You will reap a harvest if you do not give up (Gal. 6:9) loving like the Serving King…
AG

DAY 151

Can You See The Cutbacks

"We are not here to curse the darkness, but to light the candle that can guide us thru that darkness to a safe and sane future." —John F. Kennedy

He put another parable before them, saying, "The Kingdom of Heaven may be compared to a man who sowed good seed in his field, but while his men were sleeping, his enemy came and sowed weeds among the wheat and went away."

(Matthew 13:24)

Years ago, a good friend of mine and I took it upon ourselves to visit the top of Pike's Peak in Colorado Springs. By visit the top, I do not mean that we drove to the top or took the cog railway. I mean that we decided to hike on foot to the top of the mountain. The summit of the mountain stands at 14,115 feet above sea level—only 300 feet below the tallest mountain in Colorado. For two young men who grew up on the flat, fertile farmland of the Midwest, we had very little idea what to expect. Things like cutbacks, tree line, oxygen deprivation, and altitude sickness were not things we were familiar with—at least not on a personal, experiential level. Learning about those things before we went helped us handle the challenges we faced over the two days we took to ascend the peak.

In Matthew's Gospel, chapter 13, Jesus shares with His disciples about the contours, cutbacks, and celebrations of the Kingdom of Heaven. These parables are His instructions to them as He is preparing them to both live in and live out the Kingdom life He promised to them. What does the Kingdom look like? What does it mean to live in expectation and experience of the Kingdom? What obstacles can one expect along the path to the Kingdom? How will one recognize the summit? Jesus' instruction is vital for His followers to hear, digest, and apply.

Over the next two days, we're going to look more closely at verses 24-30 as they pertain to the Kingdom. However, today, let me encourage you to consider not just the content of this chapter, but in what way it can and should be approached—as a guide, an introduction, to life in God's Kingdom. Ask the Holy Spirit to help you, through the Word, to begin to see the contours, the cutbacks, and the celebrations of life in the Kingdom so that you will be ready for whatever may come your way. If you do, then even though, like all of us, you have been born and lived a long way from the Kingdom, you will not be surprised and instead be ready to embrace all that awaits you within its borders. Love on in the way of the Serving King...

AL

Seed Analysis

"I don't have a gardener, because I enjoy pulling weeds. It's hard to explain, but there is something fulfilling about pulling out a weed and knowing that you got all the roots." —Justin Harley

"He put another parable before them, saying, "The Kingdom of Heaven may be compared to a man who sowed good seed in his field, but while his men were sleeping, his enemy came and sowed weeds among the wheat and went away."

(Matthew 13:25)

In this passage, Jesus explains to His followers that the Kingdom of Heaven is like a field that contains both wheat and weeds. We read how the farmer had sown good seed in his field with the expectation of a relatively easy and uniform harvest to come. However, a jealous, bitter, and spiteful rival had sought to devastate that harvest by sowing bad seeds among the good. The ostensible genius of this plan was in the fact that both seeds would grow up together, indistinguishable from each other until it was too late. If the farm workers tried to remove the weeds once they were recognized, as the enemy hoped, they would also destroy the good crop whose roots had become entwined with the weeds. The farmer recognized this and instructed his workers to leave both in the ground until they had both ripened and borne their fruits in the harvest. Only then, would they be able to separate them—one pile for the table, the other for the furnace. In this way, the farmer outwitted his enemy.

This parable tells us many things about the contours of God's Kingdom. One of those things is that we should not be surprised that there is both good and evil in the world or that good people and evil people might grow up next to and amongst each other, even within the Church. It is all too easy to be shocked when we see the horrors of a fallen world around us, and indeed, there are many things at which to be shocked and horrified. However, as those who are living into God's Kingdom, our goal is not to eliminate all evil in the world, for there is no way to do that without also hurting the good seed. Instead, our goal is to cultivate the good seed and prepare for the harvest.

Today, ask the Holy Spirit to help you discern when it comes to the good and bad seed around you. Although it is not our task, or even without our power to remove all the evil around us, it is within our ability to cultivate and nourish the good. Pray for the Spirit to give you wisdom and strength to support the good seed while resisting the bad seed all around you. Love on in the way of the Serving King…
AL

Separation

"How can people trust the harvest, unless they see it sown?" —Mary Renault

He said to them, "An enemy has done this. To the servants said to him, 'Master, then do you want us to go and gather them?' But he said, 'No, lest in gathering the weeds you root up the wheat along with them. Let them both grow until the harvest...' (Matthew 13:28)

One of the important truths Jesus teaches in Matthew 13:24-30 is that, in spite of the fact that good and evil coexist together, there is coming a time when the two will be separated. In verse 27, when the owner's servants discovered the plot by the enemy of sowing weeds among the wheat, their immediate thought was to pull them up. The owner explained that doing so would damage the wheat in the process. The weeds of this world are plentiful and exceptionally bothersome, even painful. Yet, the temptation to deal with them ourselves, to take matters into our own hands, is to preempt God's wisdom for dealing with sin and evil, and, in the process, even do damage to the good around us. What might this look like?

Recently, a young teenage girl in my church, who has been through many difficult life experiences, shared with me how she had been hurt by a friend who had ended their relationship. When I asked why, she explained that her friend had been taught at her church to stop being friends with those who might have a negative influence in her life. Because the young teen at my church had shared with her friend about some of her past hurts, her friend decided that the negativity she had experienced was something she did not want to be associate with. Sadly, my young teen's friend misapplied the wisdom of being discerning about friendships and applied it to what should have been a positive relationship and opportunity for encouragement and growth. When we attempt, on our own, to separate the wheat from the weeds, we run the risk of doing the same.

Today, ask the Holy Spirit to help you exercise trust and caution when dealing with the evil that grows up around each of us. Jesus' words are not a call for tolerance of evil, but, instead, a reminder that judgment and removal of evil is part of His plan in His time. Allow the words of Katharina von Schlegal's powerful hymn to speak to you today::

Be still, my soul; the Lord is on thy side. Bear patiently the cross of grief or pain. Leave to they God to order and provide; In every change He faithful will remain. Be still, my soul; thy best, thy heavenly Friend through thorny ways leads to a joyful end.

TM

Hobbit Speak

"I should like to save the Shire, if I could - though there have been times when I thought the inhabitants too stupid and dull for words, and have felt that an earthquake or an invasion of dragons might be good for them." —J. R. Tolkien

The Kingdom of Heaven is like a grain of mustard seed that a man took and sowed in his field. It is the smallest of seeds, but when it has grown it is larger than the garden plants and becomes a tree, so that the birds of the air come and make nests in its branches. (Matthew 13:31-32)

Many chasing after the Serving King desire to save the shire between bouts of thinking the inhabitants too stupid or dull for words. And to be fair to hobbits who think poorly of the shire inhabitants, mere words rarely bring about the salvation of the shire; hence, the eventual assessment of too stupid and dull for words. And countless are the hours spent laboring in the realm of mere words for the sake of the too stupid and dull. But no hobbit can labor endlessly in the land of mere words without eventually succumbing to silence, the cessation of proclamation, the end of hope in mere words.

But the Word of God is no mere word, powerless and ineffectual in the mind and heart of the dull-witted. To the contrary, the Word is alive, powerful and effective in bringing about transformation in the dullest of wits. Thus, wise are those proclaimers who learn the art of proclaiming Word in the grandest forms of simplicity, casting seed recklessly across the broadest spectrum possible, knowing the intrusive power of Word. They have watched and listened to the power of the invasive Word coming from the mouth of the Serving King. More to the point, they were once in the throng of the too stupid and dull for words, until the meddlesome seed penetrated mouth and heart. Word is a powerful force of enlightenment, even for the dullest of wits.

Thus, those chasing after the Serving King soon join the chorus of proclaimers, those anxiously and readily engaged in the songs of the professed, the proclamation of Word. And so, the seed leaves the hands of the sowers invading the lives of all those within sowing distance, infected by the invasive power of the seed. The sower's job is done for now as the seed begins its invasive burrowing into the soon no longer too stupid and dull for words. It is the way of the Word from those who dare to love in the way of the Serving King…

DM

Heavenly Leaven...

"Jesus made clear that the Kingdom of God is organic and not organizational. It grows like a seed and it works like leaven: secretly, invisibly, surprisingly, and irresistibly." —Os Guinness

He told them another parable. "The Kingdom of Heaven is like leaven that a woman took and hid in three measures of flour, till it was all leavened."

(Matthew 13:33)

Leaven, or yeast, is a useful thing. It can take a dense, sloppy mixture of flour and water and make it into light, delicious bread. Just a small amount can transform a whole loaf. As Christians, our daily, faithful living out of the Kingdom is the yeast that God can use to transform our world. A gracious act of forgiveness, a sacrificial offering of help to a stranger, advocating for those who have nothing to give back in return, these acts of Christ-likeness in our world are a sharp contrast that invites others to wonder why we do it. These kindnesses, both big and small, are our witness to the world that we trust Christ as a model for our lives.

Most of the time, this is encouraging. Our faithful, unassuming lives make a real difference. Sometimes though, you are like me. Perhaps, you see the pain, the violence, the exploitation, the sin in the world, and you might wonder how much of a difference you can make in light of so much evil. This is when we need to remember something about yeast. To make bread, you mix in the yeast and give it a chance to rest, to rise. Depending on the type of bread, you might even do a couple rounds-kneading and resting, shaping and resting again. This is what gives the yeast a chance to transform the dough, creating the air bubbles that give that light airy texture and distinctive flavor.

When we get discouraged by the things around us, let us take the long view. Let us keep on doing the good work of heavenly yeast, slowly transforming our world even when it is hard to see our impact. Let us trust that when we are faithful, God is using us in ways we may never even see. Let us trust that our simple acts of Christ-likeness are making a Kingdom difference as we love in the way of the Serving King...
RS

DAY 156

Confusion Or Clarification

"Every happening, great and small, is a parable whereby God speaks to us, and the art of life is to get the message." —Malcolm Muggeridge

All these things Jesus said to the crowds in parables; indeed, He said nothing to them without a parable. This was to fulfill what was spoken by the prophet: "I will open my mouth in parables; I will utter what has been hidden since the foundation of the world." (Matt 13:34-35)

Most who read the parables of Jesus see them as amazing teachings about life and Godly living. Jesus focuses upon the idea of the Kingdom of God, what is it like. Jesus used 33 parables recorded in the Gospels. They are brief and taken from ordinary life. They often contain exaggeration and surprise to convey an unmistakable truth about life. They seem to force one to look at themselves and make a value judgment about themselves. Here, Matthew tells us that Jesus used parables exclusively when speaking to the great crowds that often followed Him. To the disciples, He often explained the parable, sometimes with great detail as in the Parable of the Sower and the Seed.

The public, as well as the Jewish leaders, were left to ponder the meaning of the parable. Sometimes the meaning was clear and biting, truth ridiculing the hypocritical actions of the Scribes and Pharisees. Mark's Gospel also contains a similar statement to the disciples about His teaching in parables. Mark's account appears to indicate the parables are intended to conceal the truth rather than clarify (Mark 4:10-12). If we take both accounts seriously, as equally valid, we may conclude that Jesus' answer may be understood in the sense that His purpose was not a simple one. The parables were intended for some listeners as a means to understand the mysteries of God and, for others, as a means to conceal this very same teaching. I submit that the ability to understand Jesus' parables lays in the condition of the heart of the listener. The open and seeking heart will be led by God's Spirit to understand the truth of the parable. The closed and spiritually rigid heart and mind will be left confused and possibly angry at what is believed about the parable, whether it is accurate or misses the meaning completely.

Today, you should read again some of your favorite parables of Jesus. What was Jesus trying to say to the people listening to Him that day? What is He saying to you today as you read and meditate upon His words? How might you love on in the ways of the Serving King...
DS

Reaping what is Sown

"Sooner or later, everyone sits down to a banquet of consequences."
—*Robert Louis Stevenson*

Then He left the crowds and went into the house. And His disciples came to Him, saying, "Explain to us the parable of the weeds of the field… Just as the weeds are gathered and burned with fire, so will it be at the end of the age. The Son of Man will send His angels, and they will gather out of His kingdom all causes of sin and all law-breakers, and throw them into the fiery furnace. In that place there will be weeping and gnashing of teeth. Then the righteous will shine like the sun in the kingdom of their Father. He who has ears, let him hear."

(Matthew 13:36-43)

The book of Matthew contains 23 parables, 7 in chapter 13 alone. Fortunately, for Christians today, Jesus' disciples often needed these elaborate analogies spelled out for them in simple language. The parable of the sower is one of many teachings about the black and white nature of Salvation. Notice that there are only two options for humanity; either they are gathered and burned with fire, or they shine like the sun in the Kingdom of their Father. There are no seeds left after the harvest, nothing left growing in the field once the reaping takes place. One way or the other, all of mankind will be gathered and judged and, in between those lines, this is a parable warning against procrastination and fair-weathered Christianity. Jesus preaches again and again that we must choose a side to fight for on the battlefield of spiritual warfare, that we cannot sit stagnant in our faith or wait to come to Christ until it is convenient for us. There is no such thing as "no-man's land" in this war. We are either for Him or against. Rather than adjusting our speech and habits to assimilate with the world, we need to stand firm and remember that what appears to be a field of flowers from afar is often nothing more than a plot of weeds.

The Bible makes it clear that Hell was not created for man. Hell was created for the devil and his angels, but when man rejects to love of God and chooses instead to follow his sin nature, he then chooses the only alternative to Christ: an eternity without the light of God.

Remind yourself daily that the reaping will come without warning. Bask in the sunshine of the Word of God and delight in the fellowship of other believers so that you may grow daily and be ready for the harvest. Love on in the ways of the Serving King…
SC

Buy The Field

"Knowledge is the treasure of a wise man." —William Penn

"The Kingdom of Heaven is like treasure hidden in a field, which a man found and covered up. Then in his joy he goes and sells all that he has and buys that field." (Matthew 13:44)

This one verse captures the difficulty most of us face in pursuing the Kingdom of God. First, the surprise at finding the treasure, recognizing it as treasure, but understanding it cannot be acquired without first freeing ourselves from all other valuables in life. And make no mistake, releasing all previous valuables from your life is much more difficult than you may have imagined. As the old saying goes, "A bird in the hand is worth two in the bush." Or, in this case, "The treasure I now own, is worth two buried in the ground."

So comes the great challenge for those who have found the treasure, the pearls of great wisdom, the teaching of the Serving King. Like the Rich Young Ruler, you have come to understand the incredible resource that is now at your fingertips waiting to be purchased by those courageous enough to 'sell all that they have' and buy the field.

And as easy as it sounds, 'selling all that they have' never comes easy; instead, few are those willing and able to make the grand transaction. Most people find the grand sell-off a bit too intimidating, more than they can handle in a single setting, a task better suited to a 'piece-by-piece' approach. Timid, they tiptoe into the waters, slowly immersing themselves into the wisdom of God, testing the waters of the buried treasure anxiously waiting in the depths God's Word.

Unfortunately, the piece-by-piece approach of those testing the waters rarely produces the desired treasure. This treasure manifests only as those radically committed, the 'sellers of everything', engage the fullness of the wisdom of God. It is they who 'buy the field' who discover the fullness of God's treasure. The others, buying only the most inexpensive pieces, rarely see the treasure made available to those who buy the field. Resist the temptation to tiptoe in. Buy the field. It is the way of those committed to loving in the way of the Serving King...
DM

An Unexpected Pearl

"You may say I'm a dreamer. But I'm not the only one I hope someday you'll join us. And the world will be as one." —John Lennon

Again, the Kingdom of Heaven is like a merchant in search of fine pearls; on finding one pearl of great value, he went and sold all that he had and bought it.
(Matthew 13:45-46)

This merchant who represented the Kingdom of Heaven was hoping to find a collection of pearls he could turn around and sell at the market. That was how he made a living, after all. But then he saw something a little different: it was a single pearl, but it had incredible value. Then he decided to do something that, according to the world around him, would have been foolish—he sold everything he had to purchase it. What good was a merchant with only one item, especially when he was so attached to it that he wouldn't sell it?

In this parable, I am reminded of the words of Paul from 1 Corinthians 1:18: "For the message about the cross is foolishness to those who are perishing, but to us who are being saved it is the power of God." The merchant in Jesus' parable gave up everything he had, even his career, because he found something he had not been looking for and he recognized it as priceless.

We must resist the temptation to say that the "pearl" in this parable is the Kingdom of Heaven, because Matthew tells us otherwise—he says that the merchant is the Kingdom of Heaven. The Kingdom of Heaven is found in the seeking, the devotion, the abandonment of the ways of the world. It is the self-giving pursuit of an unexpected goal.

The other day, the founder of a successful, Christian-oriented business shared with me how he began his career. In college, he'd planned to go to law school, but a difficult conversation with a father figure in his life forced him to recognize that the plans he'd laid—which made perfect sense from a worldly perspective—did not excite him. Because of that conversation, he chose to go into business doing something he loved, and ever since that day, he had been able to use those passions as he served others and thrived in his career.

Maybe the point of this parable is that, as followers of Christ, we are called to find a "pearl," a goal in line with the Gospel of Jesus, and we are to value it so highly that we abandon everything we have to pursue it. That is the way of great love…
RG

Deep And Wide

"Wherever the fish are, that's where we go." —Richard Wagner

"Again, the Kingdom of Heaven is like a net that was thrown into the sea and gathered fish of every kind. When it was full, men drew it ashore and sat down and sorted the good into containers but threw away the bad. So it will be at the end of the age. The angels will come out and separate the evil from the righteous and throw them into the fiery furnace. In that place there will be weeping and gnashing of teeth." (Matthew 13:47-50)

"The church is full of hypocrites, pretenders, and fakes. I love Jesus, but not the church." I've heard this rationale for skipping out on life in Christian community many times before. Better yet, I've used this rationale before, allowing it to be the reason I stayed on the fringes of church and, subsequently, my faith in the early years of my faith journey. Sadly, my premise wasn't wrong, but my conclusion certainly was.

The Ancient Greek word, σαγήνη, translated as 'net' in this passage, refers not to the typical fishing net used in those days, cast toward schools of fish for a quick haul. The word dragnet, as it is interpreted in some translations, is perhaps a more apt description. The dragnet was large, weighted, and picked up anything and everything in its path as it scraped along the bottom of the ocean floor. You'd catch fish, shrimp, and shellfish just as easily as you'd scoop up old boots, toilet seats, and your cousin's long-lost wedding ring. There's a lot of junk in there, but it's intentionally wide and indiscriminate to get as much as possible into that net. Such is the Kingdom of Heaven. Thank God, it is.

There was a time in my own life where I registered on the Kingdom of Heaven value scale somewhere between 'bad fish' and 'toilet seat', but God cast His net wide and caught me anyway. I was one of those hypocrites parading around the church like I was the real deal, when the reality within was that I was broken and sinful. Then, one day the Holy Spirit came and made me something I was not before: a new creation, a good fish.

Jesus declared that He came not for the healthy, but the sick; not the righteous, but the sinners (Luke 5:31). Let us celebrate that there are sinners in the church. There is opportunity for redemption. Judgment will have its day, but until then, let's tend the nets and claim as many fish as we can in the love of the Serving King…
DR

Trained for the Kingdom

"I've trained all my life not to be distracted by distractions." —Nik Wallenda

"Have you understood all these things?" They said to Him, "Yes." And He said to them, "Therefore every scribe who has been trained for the Kingdom of Heaven is like a master of a house, who brings out of his treasure what is new and what is old." And when Jesus had finished these parables, He went away from there. (Matthew 13:51-53)

One of my favorite parts of the Olympics is when they show short interviews with the athletes. I am not an athlete, so I am always amazed not only at the astonishing things some people can do with their bodies, but at the determination they have to get to that elite level. Physical training can be grueling. It is about repetition and pushing oneself just a little bit harder to be a little bit better. In interviews, many of these athletes will say something about training toward consistency. They not only want to be the best, they want to be able to be the best every time. Those that make it to the top do so because even their off days are really, really good. These athletes don't practice until they get it right, they practice until they can't get it wrong.

What would it look like to train ourselves for the Kingdom in this way? What if we read our Bible until we knew it thoroughly cover to cover? What if we sought God in prayer so much that we just dwelled in His presence every moment. What if we did acts of service to others until our natural response is compassion to those in need? What if we met together with other believers consistently until we longed to be with the community of faith? What if we sought peace and justice until we became a transformational influence in the world around us? What if we chased after God so consistently that we couldn't help but follow in His footprints?

This training is not easy and may be every bit as grueling as physical training. Training for the Kingdom does not rely on youthful bodies or natural talent. Training for the Kingdom is a life-long task to which we are all called. Imagine the result. Imagine what could be if our lives were lived in such a consistent, Christ-oriented way that the world around us couldn't help but be transformed into the Kingdom of God? Dare to imagine the fruit of loving in the way of the Serving King...
RS

Something Old, Something New

"Mixing one's wines may be a mistake, but old and new wisdom mix admirably."
—Bertolt Brecht

"Have you understood all these things?" They said to Him, "Yes." And He said to them, "Therefore every scribe who has been trained for the Kingdom of Heaven is like a master of a house, who brings out of his treasure what is new and what is old." And when Jesus had finished these parables, He went away from there. (Matthew 13:51-53)

There is a stereotype that exists in churches. The assumption is that there is a battle between young and old in churches, that older folks are so stuck in the past and are blind to where the church needs to go, while younger folks are caught by every new thing, drifting away without a foundation. While this certainly may be the case for some communities of faith, it doesn't need to be so.

It is also not a new phenomenon. In the early days of Christianity, there was the same tension. In Acts, we see the struggle of those who were resistant to change, wanting Gentile believers to adhere to all the Jewish laws. If it was good enough for them, certainly it would be good enough for new believers. Instead, God called the early church to embrace newcomers, allowing for contextual understandings of what their faith looked like. The early church also saw people like Marcion, who believed that the Old Testament was completely irrelevant for Christians and should be ignored in favor of what is new. Instead, we are called to study the whole of Scripture, not just a part.

So, how do we discern what is right and good? How do we bridge the generational gaps that pop up now and then? Firstly, we live so rooted in Christ that we are tuned to see where He is leading. Secondly, we do this in community with people who are different than us. When we trust that God speaks to all of His people and not just us, we can trust the discernment of our brothers and sisters who may challenge our assumptions. When we discern together, we are kept from defensiveness and pride. When we discern together, we can be faithful to what is old while embracing new realities and contexts. When we discern together, we become a vibrant part of the full, diverse body of Christ. Love on in the way of the Serving King…
RS

DAY 163

People will talk!

"Let's give them something to talk about. A little mystery to figure out. Let's give them something to talk about." —Shirley Eikhard

Coming to His hometown, He began teaching the people in their synagogue, and they were amazed. "Where did this Man get this wisdom and these miraculous powers?" they asked. "Isn't this the carpenter's son? Isn't his mother's name Mary, and aren't His brothers James, Joseph, Simon and Judas? Aren't all His sisters with us? Where then did this Man get all these things?"

(Matthew 15:54-55)

Have you ever been away from the familiarity of family, friends, home for any significant time? There's something about coming home that is comforting and terrifying all at the same time. There will certainly be a time of getting reacquainted that will have a real impact on those you know so well. Some will quickly embrace you. Others, well, they will just talk.

Jesus, returning home for the first time since His baptism, His temptation, and the beginning of His ministry, was faced with the cold, hard fact that He had changed. The person that the good people of Nazareth once knew as the son of Mary and Joseph, the oldest brother of their five sons and multiple daughters was now being called Rabbi, Teacher, Messiah, and King. They were very much shocked and probably said things like Nathaniel said when he first met Jesus, "Certainly no Kingly Messiah could come from the podunk town of Nazareth."

The Second Member of the Trinity, Jesus, emptied Himself of all that it meant to be God, and now, as a man, offered Himself wholly back to God to be filled by God through the power of the Holy Spirit at His baptism. The man Jesus was now the demonstration of what it meant to be a person filled with God and He was different! The good people of Nazareth couldn't believe what they were seeing, and let me tell you, they were talking about it.

Have you experienced the restorative infilling of the Serving King? Have you offered yourself up wholly to Him to be infilled and used by Him? What are people saying about the demonstration of this Serving King in your life? Wouldn't it be something if the subjects of His Kingdom were so close to Him, emptied of themselves, and empowered by His spirit that the same general things they said about Jesus were said about them? "She's changed!" "He's really different!" Dare to give them something to talk about as you love on in the way of the Serving King…
DC

DAY 164

Seeing Clearly

"The only thing worse than being blind is having sight but no vision."
—*Hellen Keller*

And they took offense at Him. But Jesus said to them, "A prophet is not without honor except in his own town and in his own home." And He did not do many miracles there because of their lack of faith. (Matthew 13:57-58)

When Jesus encountered the blind man in Luke, Chapter 18, He asked him, "What do you want Me to do for you?" The man answered, "Lord I want to see!" Jesus then said to him, "Receive your sight, your faith has healed you."

In this myriad of strange and unusual events we call life, it is easy to dismiss or even be offended by things and people we do not understand. We have the tendency to question the motivation and intention of people who might even be trying their best to help us or others. "Who are you to tell me?" Sound familiar?

The contrast between the response of the people of Jesus' hometown, whom He freely offered the gift of His presence, and the blind man, desperate to truly see, is dramatic. The hometown crowd were so close-minded and rigid they could not fathom someone, who they knew so well, having such a life-transforming experience, the kind of experience that changes a carpenter into a rabbi. They missed the significance of who Jesus really was.

The blind man, on the other hand, was so desperate for sight, he was completely open to the possibility that the One who stood before him was the Son of God. He didn't miss Jesus and, as a result, received his sight. In fact, it is such a drastic contrast that the Bible says because of the lack of faith in the people of Jesus' hometown, He just could not help them. Sometimes a lack of physical sight is not the real blindness at all. Clearly, the blind man saw realities the townsfolk could not imagine.

May we, the modern-day people of God, always be open to the movement of God around us, even when it is shockingly unusual, occurring in the lives of the least likely people. May we always be open enough and have the desperate humility to cry out, "Lord, I want to see clearly, give us sight so we never miss You." Risk seeing what others miss as you love on in the way of the Serving King…
DC

The Cost

"I always wanted to be Robin Hood or John the Baptist when I was growing up."
—*Bear Grylis*

Prompted by her mother, she said, "Give me the head of John the Baptist here on a platter." And the king was sorry, but because of his oaths and his guests he commanded it to be given. He sent and had John beheaded in the prison, and his head was brought on a platter and given to the girl, and she brought it to her mother. And his disciples came and took the body and buried it, and they went and told Jesus. (Matthew 14:1-12)

John the Baptist is one of the most interesting people in Scripture. I believe he falls in a category with Elijah, Elisha, and Jeremiah, men who stood up for the Word of God regardless of what anyone liked, desired, or wanted. John was the first one to declare, "The Lamb of God who will take away the sins of the World" (John 1:29). And he was honored in baptizing Jesus at the river Jordan.

Tragically, John's life ended less than gloriously; but, he understood how costly following Jesus could be. "Then Jesus said to His disciples, if anyone wants to follow in My footsteps he must give up all right to himself, take up his cross and follow Me. For the man who wants to save his life will lose it; but the man who loses his life for My sake will find it. For what good is it for a man to gain the whole world at the price of his own soul? What could a man offer to buy back his soul once he had lost it?" (Matthew 16:25-26) Not surprisingly, John passed the toughest of tests: Death because of his allegiance to Jesus.

Unlike John, today's Christians often struggle standing tall with Jesus. I find that the one who gives his heart and soul, and sometimes his life, is a person who follows in the footsteps of John. Sometimes, it is the cost of following Jesus. It is a hard thing to do, but it is the only thing we can do if we are genuinely Christian. I know some would say, "That is a lot to ask of someone, to give up everything, for the sake of Jesus." Indeed. Yet, my response would be, "Jesus gave up everything for us, it would be an honor to do the same for Him." John knew the cost of loving in the way of the Serving King. Perhaps, we too can love in the way of the Serving King...
TM

The Guardian

"There are times when fear is good. It must keep its watchful place at the heart's controls." —Aeschylus

And though he wanted to put Him to death, he feared the people, because they held him to be a prophet. (Matthew 14:5)

It is a glorious moment, foolish, but glorious, nonetheless, freedom; no longer tethered to the guardian of the heart. The guardian, long-entrenched at the front of the heart, has protected the fool content to run this way and that were it not for the guardian, relentless in protecting the fool from the folly of his ways. The guardian, the "fear of God," the final watchman for the heart, stands guard as the fool frivolously considers another step. But "fear of God," the final restraint, wains as the wisdom of God fades in the distance, and the fool listens to the many voices drowning out the guardian. Herod learns the hard way.

Soon, the fool, cocky in the present moment, dancing with the many, liberated from the sense of the Serving King's abiding presence, cuts loose the "fear of God," freed to embark on a life released from the Servant King's nagging presence. More importantly, detached from the guardian, "fear of God" no longer restraining the feet of the fool. What a glorious moment this will be for the fool as the many welcome another player to the treacherous game of life freed from the "fear of God." Herod joins Herodias in the dance of folly.

Alas, the moment, short or long as it may be, is nothing more than an illusionary condition, fleeting at best, unable to sustain the promised well-being, chaos, and destruction hiding in the shadows, yet soon to arrive. But the fool, no longer looking ahead, no longer restrained by the guardian, freed from fear in "…its watchful place at the heart's controls," runs recklessly into the pleasure of the fleeting moment. And, the joy of the moment for the fool, as the guardian mourns the impending chaos lurking in the shadows. But the guardian is not dead, even in the profound silence, ever the gentle breeze, waiting for the opportune moment to return to its intended post, gently speaking into the being and doing of the fool lost in the noise of the crowd, chaos ever spreading as the fool skips along. Still, the guardian patiently waits for the fool to return home. There is still time for Herod. It is never too late to begin loving in the way of the Serving.

DM

A Voice

"I want to be prophetic and take stands and stand with those on the margins, and I want to laugh as much as I can." —Greg Boyle

And his disciples came and took the body and buried it, and they went and told Jesus. (Matthew 14:12)

Have you ever heard it asked, "why do bad things happen to good people?" I often consider this when contemplating the fate of John the Baptist. Perhaps, Isaiah is referring to John in his mind as he declared, "For this is he who was spoken of by the prophet Isaiah, when he said the voice of one crying in the wilderness: Prepare the way of the Lord; make his paths straight" (Isaiah 40:3).

Preparing the way is the fruit of thinking, feeling, and deciding. It is a simple choice; where are we going to stand in that moment of decision? Scripture declares; "Do you not know that if you present yourselves to anyone as obedient slaves, you are slaves of the one whom you obey, either of sin, which leads to death, or of obedience, which leads to righteousness" (Romans 6:16)? John was preparing people for the fact that Jesus was coming to make a way for redemption, but that the cost would be great: Jesus very life!

Jesus did His part, but said that any who would follow Him would need to pick up their own cross. Jesus said, "You will be hated by all for My name's sake. But the one who endures to the end will be saved" (Matthew 10:22). John the Baptist knew the cost would be high, but he trusted in the One he first declared as "…the Lamb of God who was to take away the sin of the world" (John 1:29). Paul the Apostle also knew the price. He, too, paid the price for standing for Jesus. He encouraged Timothy, "Of this Gospel I was appointed a herald and an apostle and a teacher. That is why I am suffering as I am. Yet this is no cause for shame, because I know whom I have believed and am convinced that he is able to guard what I have entrusted to him until that day" (II Timothy 1:11-12).

Being a voice in the wilderness of life has a price, but you and I do not need to fear tomorrow, because we rest in the hands of the One who holds tomorrow. Dare to join the thong of those who have gone before us in loving in the way of the Serving King…
TM

Crowds

"I don't think even ungodly people realize what a society would be like that had no godly influence at all." —Joyce Meyer

Now when Jesus heard this, He withdrew from there in a boat to a desolate place by Himself. But when the crowds heart it, they followed Him on foot from the towns. When He went ashore He saw a great crowd, and He had compassion on them and healed their sick. (Matthew 14:13-15)

The many, too exhausted from the demands of day-to-day life, the concerns of work and family, rarely find time to hear God. Thus, the temptation to simply do as the crowd seems to be doing. The many trust in doing good as the means of right relationship with God. And so, religious communities have little trouble finding adherents to well-established ways of doing and working for those too busy to hear. Be good and follow the crowd.

But the few, daring to pause from all the activity, the grind of daily existence and patterns of worship created long ago by well-intentioned hard workers, seek out the Serving King, determined to hear from Him for a more personal instruction on being and doing. It is only those who hear God who ever face the difficult decision to believe God. And yes, for those daring to hear God deep into the journey, believing will be trickier than you may suspect. Yet, here they come on foot to hear from Jesus.

In the early stages of chasing after the Serving King, the voice of God seemingly rarely startles the listener; instead, providing the elementary basics all newborns are prepared to handle. But later, deep into the journey, the Serving King begins to make known challenging particulars for those willing to pry deeper into conversations with the Serving King. Like Abraham, the particulars become ever more challenging, impacting family and friend alike, influencing society and culture. And so, the ungodly, who rarely "...realize what a society would be like that had no godly influence at all," suddenly discover the presence of His ambassadors, those most reflecting His way of being and doing.

For in the end, it is those who believe God who impact society in the most powerful ways of all. But you can't believe until you first slow down, seek Him out, and listen carefully. Only those in the crowd who actually hear will know how to love on in the ways of the Serving King... DM

Following The Crowd

"It is easier to serve God without a vision, easier to work for God without a call, because then you are not bothered by what God requires; commonsense is your guide, veneered over with Christian sentiment. You will be more prosperous and successful, more leisure hearted, if you never realize the call of God."
—*Oswald Chambers*

Now when Jesus heard this, He withdrew from there in a boat to a desolate place by Himself. But when the crowds heart it, they followed Him on foot from the towns. When He went ashore He saw a great crowd, and He had compassion on them and healed their sick. (Matthew 14:13-15)

Those who have been 'called' by the King soon discover trekking after Him is not nearly so leisurely and 'spontaneous' as we would like to believe. Since few of the 'sheep' are genuinely 'called' but, rather, have simply 'wandered' into the pen, they will not understand the few who were 'called' and the strange way in which the 'called-out ones' describe their allegiance to the Serving King.

Nor will the flock, those meandering along behind the Shepherd, understand the power the Shepherd seems to have over those who have 'heard' His call; more than that, have been 'claimed' by Him, following His every direction. The 'called-out ones' will indeed battle from time to time a sense of envy concerning the vast majority of the flock who have such a leisurely approach to life and obedience to the King. The 'called-out ones' may indeed notice the 'other' sheep do indeed seem to have a "...more prosperous and successful, more leisure-hearted..." trek after the King. He even feeds them!

But for the child of the Serving King who has been 'called out', a new realization begins to take root in the soil of the soul, an understanding changing everything, a new way of being and doing so profound it renders the 'life of leisure' moot, forgotten, no longer desired or sought after. That, of course, is the 'sign', the testimony, the proof, the verification, you have indeed been 'called'. Your life, that journey of leisure and prosperity, no longer has any value at all. This 'valueless life' cannot be manufactured, willed into being, mandated into existence; to the contrary, it is simply the by-product of 'loving' the One who has called you to "...follow Me" and "...feed My sheep." Love feeds the sheep who meander into the pen...

DM

Feed The Sheep

"The process of being made broken bread and poured-out wine means that you have to be the nourishment for other souls until they learn to feed on God. They must drain you to the dregs. Be careful that you get your supply, or before long you will be utterly exhausted. Before other souls learn to draw on the life of the Lord Jesus direct, they have to draw on it through you; you have to be literally 'sucked', until they learn to take their nourishment from God." —Oswald Chambers

Now when it was evening, the disciples came to Him and said, "This is a desolate place, and the day is over; send the crowds away to go into the villages and buy food for themselves." But Jesus said to them, "They need not go away; you give them something to eat." (Matthew 14:15-16)

No child of the King, including the disciples, has any concept of what 'feeding my sheep' will exact from them over the years of trekking after the Serving King. Hearing the tales of exhaustion from others will do little to prepare you for the toll 'feeding my sheep' will take upon your life. The trail is littered with the casualties of those who have fallen by the wayside utterly exhausted and spent, having attempted to feed others while not being fed.

Pausing to be fed is extremely problematic for a generation of followers who have long feasted on fast food, prepared to be devoured on the go, consumed while engaged in a myriad of activity. Rarely does God provide nourishment on the fly or even in the gathering of the many; instead, dining with God is almost always a solitary affair. You will be tempted to consume the appetizer, that gathering with the 'saints' in praise and worship, over and over again. But eating with the crowd rarely provides the nourishment you truly need. However, you cannot find the sustenance needed to 'feed my sheep' while in the frenzy of the many, delightful as that menu may be; no, the sustenance needed to 'feed my sheep' can only be found in solitary dining with the Living God.

You will need to be mindful of the needed frequency of those solitary moments with God. Those who often feed the many need to be especially sensitive to refueling, taking in more than you are giving out. Resist the temptation to bask in the 'feeding of others', a constant threat. Find those needed moments to dine alone in the presence of the Living God. The road, littered with casualties, has too many victims already. Loving like the Serving King will always mandate feeding His sheep...
DM

DAY 171

Tending Sheep

"Spend it (love) out. Don't testify how much you love Me, don't profess about the marvelous revelation you have had, but—"Feed My sheep." And Jesus has some extraordinarily funny sheep, some bedraggled, dirty sheep, some awkward butting sheep, some sheep that have gone astray!" —Oswald Chambers

And He said to them, "Bring them here to Me." Then He ordered the crowds to sit down on the grass, and taking the five loaves and the two fish, He looked up to heaven and said a blessing. Then He broke the loaves and gave them to the disciples, and the disciples gave them to the crowds. And they all ate and were satisfied. (Matthew 14:18-20)

The business of 'tending' someone else's sheep is a messy business indeed; primarily, because you have so little to say about the condition and kind of sheep the 'other' keeps. That will take some getting used to, especially if you intend to care for the kind of sheep Jesus keeps, those 'extraordinarily' sheep who have found the Shepherd or, better yet, whom the Shepherd has found. They will often leisurely follow after the Serving King who keeps them fed.

You will be tempted to think, "They must be like Jesus, after all, they are His sheep," but you wrong, and that is why 'tending His sheep' is so very difficult. More times than not, they are nothing like Him. His standard is so very low that almost any sheep, ok, any sheep, can gain access to His pens, can follow along, and sit at His feet. That will take some getting used to. His sheep, for all the instructions on how to be like Him, remain far too often very much unlike Him. Thus, the idea of loving them out of 'natural' love toward them is just highly unlikely. Hence, the 'examination' by Him to make sure your love for Him is enough to sustain you while you are 'spending it' toward sheep who are very often so preoccupied with 'life in general' and 'grazing' to even notice you are 'spending it' on them.

Thus, you really understand His concern in determining if you really, really, really, love Him. You simply will not be able to sustain tending this group of "...extraordinarily funny sheep, some bedraggled sheep, dirty sheep, some awkward butting sheep, some sheep that have gone astray!" Then that startling moment of clarity, that comprehension that cannot be side-stepped, that horrific truth piercing the heart, arrives yet again. You, the one called to tend the sheep, are one of that motley flock. Nonetheless, keep loving and feeding…

DM

What are you waiting for?

"High achievers spot rich opportunities swiftly, make big decisions quickly and move into action immediately. Follow these principles and you can make your dreams come true". —Robert Schuller

Immediately He made the disciples get into the boat and go before Him to the other side, while He dismissed the crowds. (Matthew 14:22)

With a God-given task ahead of you, are you tempted to procrastinate or move? Jesus moved with immediacy. He didn't wait. He had a lesson to teach. Immediately, He compelled with urgency (so says the Greek) His disciples to get into the boat and get moving. He did this while still dismissing the crowds. Jesus did not have the time or inclination to lollygag.

The word immediately appears 21 times in Matthew. It describes Jesus' actions eight times and the actions of His disciples four times. Jesus was baptized and immediately came up out of the water. Some people choose to spend a few extra seconds under the waters of baptism. Sometimes the pastor demands it. But Jesus shot right back up. He had a God-given, Spirit-led mission to fulfill, and He would not be deterred. Jesus moved with Godly urgency.

Jesus expected the same disposition in His disciples. When Jesus called His first disciples, the four fishermen, immediately they left their livelihoods and followed Him. What about you?

When Jesus calls you to a God-given task, do you move with a Godly urgency? Or do you dawdle? Our reasons for procrastinating abound. I am afraid. I am tired. I am sinful. I am busy. I am ill-equipped. I am distracted. That may be. But the Lord expects greater from us, because He has placed greater in us. Despite our failures, He has not left us unequipped. He has given us His Holy Spirit. And with His Spirit, all things are possible.

The Spirit gives us power, provision, remembrance, transformation, and gifts. The Spirit produces in us His good character (the Fruit of the Spirit). We are not alone. Therefore, expect better things of yourself in the Lord. And move with Godly immediacy. His power and provision are with you as you keep on loving like the Serving King...
VC

Take A Seat!

"Walking with a friend in the dark is better than walking alone in the light."
—*Helen Keller*

And after He had dismissed the crowds, He went up on the mountain by Himself to pray. When evening came, He was there alone, but the boat by this time was a long way from the land, beaten by the waves, for the wind was against them. And in the fourth watch of the night He came to them, walking on the sea.

(Matthew 14:23-25)

Jesus moved with Godly urgency in everything He did; that is, except when it came to spending alone time with His Father. When it came to alone time, what we might call devotional time, Jesus slowed down and took a seat. Does alone time with God hold that place of prominence in your life? What does your devotional life look like?

Three times in Matt. 14:22-33, Jesus acted immediately. It is the adverb that characterizes the action of Jesus' walk on the water. But in the midst of that action, Jesus dismissed everyone (with prejudice), His disciples and the crowds, to spend time alone with God.

By my reckoning, Jesus spent eight hours alone with God in prayer, give or take an hour. Dinner (with 5,000 guests) was likely over by the end of the first watch. And Jesus approached His disciples on the water in the fourth watch. When was the last time you spent eight hours alone with God? Was that in a sitting, in a week, in a month, or in a year?

Why did Jesus spend extravagant alone time with God? He certainly wasn't concerned about being heard. See Jesus' teaching about prayer in Matthew 6 (do not pray like the pagans). However, He was conscientious about the primacy of intimacy with the Father (He who sees what is done in secret will reward you).

"Seek first the Kingdom of God" is a fundamental principle at work here, as is "Love the Lord your God with all your heart." At the heart of a thriving Christian life is a robust relationship with the Lord. That relationship begins with a serious prayer life. That relationship begins with well-guarded alone time with the Lord. But it only begins there. From alone time flows power. From alone time flows guidance. And from alone time flows action, the same action that characterized the life of Jesus and His disciples. So, press into alone time with the Lord. And be prepared for an empowered life of loving like the Serving King...
VC

Take Two!

"Those who do not remember the past are condemned to repeat it."
—George Santayana

Peter got out of the boat and walked on the water and came to Jesus. But when he saw the wind, he was afraid, and beginning to sink he cried out, "Lord, save me. Jesus immediately reached out His hand and took hold of him, saying to him, "O you of little faith, why did you doubt?" And when they got into the boat, the wind ceased. (Matthew 12:28-32)

This isn't the first time the disciples have encountered Jesus on the Sea of Galilee. In Chapter 8, Jesus led His disciples onto the lake precisely in time for a surprise storm. Jesus was intent on testing His disciples' faith in Him. More than that, Jesus was intent on building His disciples' faith in Him. So, He fashioned a maritime test. And His clever catechism brought about its intended result. His disciples responded, "What sort of Man is this, that even winds and sea obey Him?"

But Jesus' testing and building of our faith in Him is not a one-time event. It is an ongoing series of events. And He often takes us back to familiar places and settings to build on lessons previously begun. So, Jesus again meets with His disciples on the Sea of Galilee. "Take heart; it is I." Take two! Notice the straightforward recapitulation of the action (see Matthew 8:23-27). The disciples sink. They are afraid. They cry out, "Save us Lord." Jesus rebukes their lack of faith. Jesus rescues them. The wind ceases. The structure and setting are very similar.

But a second lesson is meant to be more than just a recapitulation of the first. It is meant to build upon a lesson already learned (or in process), much as teachers do in following a developmental course of study. Much is the same. But something is different this go round. Jesus presents an opportunity for His disciple to willingly step into the action. In Take One, Peter was thrust into testing. In Take Two, sensing the recapitulation, Peter thrusts himself into the testing. He is seeking to love Jesus enough to walk on water! Keep loving!

When Jesus leads you into a time of testing and building, don't be surprised by recapitulations. You have already gained (or are gaining) skills from your first encounter. Look for opportunities to exercise what you have learned. And eagerly anticipate the new skills you will gain. "Take heart; it is I." Do not be afraid as you dare to love like Me...
VC

Constant companions

"The greatest test of courage on earth is to bear defeat without losing heart."
—Robert Green Ingersoll

And those in the boat worshiped Him, saying, "Truly You are the Son of God."
(Matthew 12:33)

Do you expect Jesus to put you to the test? How seriously? How often? Jesus put His disciples to the test repeatedly. As His disciple, you can confidently expect the same treatment. How does that make you feel? Does that encourage you?

The testing and building of your faith is a gift from Jesus. Testing gives you a means to measure your progress. Building ensures you will not long be disappointed with your progress. Testing and building are constant companions on your journey towards holiness. Without them, you become stunted in your growth in grace. So learn to welcome testing and building. Peter did.

In Take One, Peter (together with the other disciples) was struck with dread by a fast-acting furious storm (likely, a wet microburst). He knew the lake and understood the peril. So he (and the others) cried out to Jesus, and Jesus saved them. Peter learned that day to trust Jesus in times of peril.

In Take Two, Peter (together the other disciples) was again embattled by wind and waves. But this time, he stepped out in faith into increased peril, because he had learned to trust Jesus during perilous times. He doubted and sank. But he was encouraged by his progress in the faith. He wasn't the only one who grew in faith. The entire crew moved from "What sort of man is this, that even winds and sea obey Him?" to "Truly You are the Son of God."

Growth is the obvious effect of testing and building. Why would you not want this in your walk with Jesus? Why would Jesus, who loves you, withhold it from you?

It behooves you to accept that testing and building are your constant companions in this walk of faith. Even more, it edifies you to embrace testing and building as your welcome companions when learning to love as the Serving King…

VC

Jesus is in the Neighborhood

"Nothing is so healing as the human touch." —Bobby Fischer

When they had crossed over, they landed at Gennesaret. And when the men of that place recognized Jesus, they sent word to all the surrounding country. People brought all their sick to Him and begged Him to let the sick just touch the edge of His cloak, and all who touched it were healed.   (Matthew 14:34-36)

Have you seen Jesus? Have you recognized Him as the God who heals? If so, have you sent word to everybody that He is here? Jesus' reputation preceded Him, and He was long awaited for by the people in Gennesaret. It's as if they knew exactly what they would do when they heard He was close. Word went out and everybody even remotely nearby brought their sick loved ones to Jesus. They had such faith! They didn't need a conversation with Him, they knew He carried the power to heal. It simply came out of Him onto everyone who touched Him. It was His very nature! Nothing He conjured up or determined He would give to some and not others. They didn't beg Jesus to heal the sick, they begged Him to let them touch the edge of His cloak. They knew it was in His power to heal, and He didn't turn anyone down.

Sometimes we over-complicate our relationship with Jesus. We place a lot of emphasis on maintaining our conversation with Him through prayer. As important as prayer is, how often do we seek to simply be in His presence and receive whatever He has to offer? The Bible is clear: God is the same yesterday, today, and tomorrow. He has not changed since His visit to Gennesaret. Do we go to Him expecting that He really is the same Jesus that healed everyone who touched His cloak?

If you believe that Jesus died for your sins and conquered death in order that you might have life, then Jesus has entered your neighborhood! In fact, He is living inside you. You get to touch His heart. How much more powerful could that be than His cloak, an outer garment made by human hands? Reach inside and touch the heart of God! Be in His presence. Receive what He has to offer today. And then, call the people of the town and let them know. The God who heals and redeems is in your neighborhood as you love on like the Serving King…
MR

Patterns Of Goodness...

"...there is no regeneration, no being born again into the Kingdom in which Christ lives, but only the idea that He is our Pattern. In the New Testament Jesus Christ is savior long before He is pattern. Today He is being dispatched as the figurehead of a religion, a mere Example". —Oswald Chambers

Then the Pharisees and scribes came to Jesus from the Jerusalem and said, "Why do Your disciples break the traditions of the elders? For they do not wash their hands when they eat?" (Matthew 15:1-2)

The temptation to follow a mere pattern of the Serving King, a valiant effort to act good, rather than be good, is a constant threat in a culture desperate to enhance the good behavior of its citizens, long stripped of the necessary ingredients for being good, the invasive presence of the Holy Spirit into the not good of our being. Acting good, according to the pattern, is far simpler than actually becoming good.

Jesus had much to say about the pretense of following a pattern of goodness, "Woe to you, scribes and Pharisees, hypocrites! For you are like whitewashed tombs, which outwardly appear beautiful, but within are full of dead people's bones and all uncleanness" (Matthew 23:27). Such is the good of those content in merely following His way of doing, yet void of His way of being. The being, always meant to be the footing of His way of doing, can only be when His Spirit has taken up residence, regenerating the old being into His new being.

The fruit of being renders the need for a pattern moot. Good needs no pattern to follow; it simply does what it is. Hence, there is no need for Law, braille for the blind, pointing this way and that, for those unable to navigate life by the good dwelling within. And you will be tempted from time-to-time to simply follow the pattern of Jesus, His way of doing, but you must resist, searching instead for a higher way, for His way of 'being'. Once found, generated by the Spirit's presence, patterns will be a thing of the past. You will finally be free to leave the 'braille' behind, striking out into the world that is now yours, long removed from the world of His patterns entrenched in a culture now invisible to the modern eye, buried in the ruins of a culture long deceased. You are free to generate new patterns, inspired by His being, creating new ways of being good, relevant to this world of the present moment. Fear not. Being good is what He had in mind all along as you love on in the ways of the Serving King...

DM

Commands

"Bow your neck to His yoke alone, and to no other yoke whatever; and be careful to see that you never bind a yoke on others that is not placed by Jesus Christ. It takes God a long time to get us out of the way of thinking that unless everyone sees as we do, they must be wrong. That is never God's view. There is only one liberty, the liberty of Jesus at work in our conscience enabling us to do what is right."

—*Oswald Chambers*

Then the Pharisees and scribes came to Jesus from Jerusalem and said, "Why do Your disciples break the tradition of the elders? For they do not wash their hands when they eat." He answered them, "And why do you break the commandment of God for the sake of your tradition?   (Matthew 15:1-3)

It is a dramatic thing for a child trekking after the Serving King when they finally, authentically, begin to hear the voice of God offering opportunities to go 'this way' or 'that way'. For those who hear the voice of God clearly, dramatically, beyond a shadow of a doubt, a horrible temptation arises to place the command of God on the lives of those around you, who likewise seek the Living God. You will be tempted to think, "If God desires this or that thing for my life, then surely God will want it for everyone else as well." Thus, the temptation to become God's mailman for the community around you, a modern-day Pharisee checking on the behavior of others.

Rest assured, the job of 'God's mailman' was filled long ago. The Holy Spirit, the communicating arm of the Godhead, accepted the responsibility to deliver the wisdom and desires of God to each one trekking after the Serving King. But neither are you called to silence. Instead, those trekking with the Serving King are called to 'pick up their yoke' and follow alongside Him, sharing with all who ask, 'the kind of yoke that Jesus has given'.

Beware the greater threat, the temptation to turn away from Jesus to examine the 'yoke' that He has placed on another. If you pause to look, ponder the yoke of another, He will see your transgression, your hesitancy, and, indeed, you will hear those painful words, "And why do you break the commandment of God?" Never place your 'yoke' on the life of another. Further, never compare 'yokes' with someone else. Understand God loves each one so personally that every 'yoke' is custom-made to lead each trekker to that place God has uniquely created. Pick up your 'yoke', focus on Jesus, and love on in the way of the Serving King...
DM

The Heart

"I am a slave to your love. Well, more like indentured servant." —Jarod Kinz

"This people honors Me with their lips, but their heart if far from Me; in vain they worship Me, teaching as doctrines the commandments of men."

(Matthew 15:8-9)

Obedience from the heart goes by another name littering the pages of literature across the ages. And once smitten, the heart knows no defense against the ultimate master, destined for a life of slavery, the heart joyfully surrenders to a new sovereign. Such is the nature of love, a master of the highest kind, rendering all efforts at rebellion moot. Love easily conquers even the most rebellious spirit. But love must be authentic. Obedience lacking authentic love is never pleasing to God. Lip-service, eloquent as it may be, is worthless without love.

Thus, love is a master stronger than any other, fiercely competitive, reckless in expression, willing to pay any price to fulfill the longings of the beloved. And the heart, once captured, knows no other interest in life, liberated from all previous masters, solely focused on the calling of the beloved. So the heart becomes a slave of righteousness. And with each passing revelation, love grows as the true nature of the beloved becomes clearer and clearer, ever deepening the slave to righteousness. There is no turning back for the heart smitten by God. This is no mere lip service.

But sin is a jealous, scorned lover, determined to regain mastery of the heart in the days yet ahead. Armed with a litany of distractions, sin will make grand efforts to recapture the heart, but this a battle long lost. There can be no retaking of the heart once it has been captured by love for the Serving King. Sin conquers lip-service, but never love.

And the fruit of love, righteousness of the highest kind, will blossom in the life of those radically in love with the Serving King. Sin, once the ruling master of the heart, fades into memory, a distant faint recollection of a life that once was but is no more. And then the grandest discovery of all. The Beloved has loved you all along. Now you are free to love in the ways of the Serving King…

DM

What Comes Out

"The soul of sweet delight, can never be defiled." —William Blake

"...it is not what goes into the mouth that defiles a person, but what comes out of the mouth that defiles a person." (Matthew 15:11)

There is a famous scene in the 1970s version of the film, Charlie and the Chocolate Factory, in which the children who are taking a tour of the famous factory are led into a room by Willie Wonka, the eccentric owner of the factory. In this particular room, they are introduced to a large machine that fills most of the space in the room, complete with whirring engines, bells and whistles, and many moving parts. The children walk the length of the machine and wait with eager expectation for what is sure to be a gigantic piece of candy that is the product of all of this noise. In the end, all of the fancy machinations produce a small gumdrop. To Wonka's credit, the small gumdrop was an "everlasting gobstopper," which he purports to be a candy that maintains its flavor and its size forever. However, the amount of hard work this large machine puts forth for such a small result rightly seems like overkill to the children and parents who are watching.

In Matthew's Gospel, Jesus is consistently disappointed that the Pharisees, with all of their work and their outward traditions and efforts, produce so little real fruit in regard to the true ways of God. They put so much "into" their religious work, but very little is produced after all of that work. This is because their focus is on the wrong things. For example, the Pharisees were extremely cautious about dietary laws, seeing these as a key measurement of one's holiness.

However, Jesus reminds them and us that the real focus of holiness is what comes out—what is produced in regard to living out the ways of God in the world. All of their efforts looked impressive in regard to the meticulous ways in which they measured what they took in, but the results were tiny, and the ways of Jesus produce an abundant harvest of righteous that actually pleases God and changes the world. Such is the productivity of those who love like the Serving King...
CC

God's Least Favorite Thing

"Never forget that everything Hitler did in Germany was legal."
—*Martin Luther King Jr.*

"He answered, 'Every plant that My heavenly Father has not planted will be rooted up. . . .'" (Matthew 15:13)

An old cartoon during World War II shows men on the assembly line testing large shells (bullets). They were testing them with a hammer, and the ones that didn't explode were marked as "duds." The poor guy who was using the hammer flinched every time and seemed glad to cast aside the rejected rounds.

The content of God's "reject" list would surprise many people. At first, it would appear that all kinds of sinners would be on the "dud" list. However, throughout the Bible, and expressed here in this passage, we find that God's least favorite thing is legalism. Legalism occurs when we attempt to use our actions—our "works"—to earn the grace of God. Legalism focuses upon our own definitions of goodness instead of God's. It causes us to miss the ultimate goodness of God by substituting our own measurements for His. There is only one remedy for legalism: trading our human-centered ways for God's priorities.

Anytime legalism rears its head in the Bible, God marks it a "dud." It is, in the words of Jesus, "a plant that my Heavenly Father has not planted." Why? It is because God has His own definition of goodness, of success, and of holiness. When we try and substitute our own definitions, this evokes the anger of God, and this is what makes God's "reject" list. Our sin can be conquered, but only by God's holiness, and not our own.

God's least favorite thing may be legalism, but His favorite thing…is us! Loving like the Serving King cures even the worst case of legalism… CC

DAY 182

Out of Hiding

"Love makes your soul crawl out from its hiding place." —Zora Neale Hurston

"But what comes out of the mouth proceeds from the heart, and this defiles a person. For out of the heart come evil thoughts, murder, adultery, sexual immorality, theft, false witness, slander. These are what defile a person. But to eat with unwashed hands does not defile anyone." (Matthew 15:19-20)

Whenever the New Testament uses the word "heart," there is a secret involved. The word 'kardia' (from where we get "cardio") is not simply about the muscle that pumps blood through our bodies. It has the connotation of the hidden places of human intimacy. At times in Scripture, we read about Jesus "knowing their hearts," and about others who plan secret things or even treasure things "in their hearts."

So, when Jesus is talking about our actions—good or bad—He notes that the "heart" is the place where this begins (see 15:19). The Good News is that Jesus is not concerned about simply a "surface level" commitment. Nor is His redemptive work limited to a surface level transformation! When we follow Jesus as Lord, He deals with the most intimate and even secretive areas of our lives, not to shame us, but to transform us. He makes the broken places whole, from the inside out.

He is willing to help us face the secret place where sin originates. We, like the religious leaders Jesus confronts in this passage, often dwell on matters that are less important than genuine "heart-level" transformation. Jesus calls them and us to look beyond surface issues and deal with matters of the heart. He loves us at the most intimate level!

Just as a sinful heart is the root of all kinds of sin, including those listed in this passage, a transformed heart begins to produce what Paul would later call the "fruit of the Spirit." The inner transformation flows outward, expressing a transformed life of devotion to God and service to others as we love like the Serving King...
CC

The Good and Bad of Tradition

"The modernity of yesterday is the tradition of today, and the modernity of today will be tradition tomorrow." —Jose Andres

"But what comes out of the mouth proceeds from the heart, and this defiles a person. For out of the heart come evil thoughts, murder, adultery, sexual immorality, theft, false witness, slander. These are what defile a person. But to eat with unwashed hands does not defile anyone." (Matthew 15:19-20)

Everyone has traditions. Traditions are what bind us together in community and assist us in passing along something of importance to future generations. Even churches who say that they are "non-traditional," are actually practicing a tradition of being non-traditional!

With all the good that comes from traditions, as much as they are part of our reality, and as much as Jesus Himself evoked tradition positively on occasion, we see here a place where Jesus warns of the dangers of tradition not accompanied by devotion.

The Pharisees seemed to have a habit of justifying sinful behavior, or at least of skewing their priorities, by citing their participation in certain traditions. In the case of the passage we are focusing upon, their current focus was upon the disciples and others who did not properly attend to ritual washing before meals. This was simply one of many ways the religious leaders of Jesus' day sought to undermine the work that He and His disciples were doing. The problem was that, even despite their dogged devotion to rituals and tradition, many of the Pharisees and other religious leaders were not bearing righteous fruit. In other words, they were not demonstrating devotion to God and to God's ways, even though they were going through the motions of proper ritual and tradition. This, as Jesus points out, is an example of how tradition can become a way of hiding from the transformation to which God calls us.

May our traditions point us toward the ways of God and His transforming grace as we keep loving like the Serving King!
CC

Overflowing Abundance

"Nurturing an inclusive culture begins in the family. Home is the first place to foster openness and a culture of inclusion." —Alain Dehaze

And Jesus went away from there and withdrew to the district of Tyre and Sidon. And behold, a Canaanite woman from that region came out and was crying, "Have mercy on me, O Lord, Son of David; my daughter is severely oppressed by a demon." But He did not answer her a word. And His disciples came and begged Him, saying, "Send her away, for she is crying out after us."

(Matthew 15:21-23)

This woman is petitioning the Lord. Society has deemed her unworthy of grace. For the Messiah has come for Israel, not this Gentile woman. But here, we find a non-Jew causing a scene and not for her own account. We see her having faith and calling upon a man she sees as the Savior for her daughter. This mother has asked mercy upon herself, but for the sake of another, her daughter. This is true empathy. She is selflessly asking for an act of grace, a miracle. The woman is intervening for someone who cannot do it for themselves, out of love and compassion for another.

In this story, she will speak to Christ three times, but she only receives two replies. This first request is answered with silence from Jesus. She already called out, "Lord, Son of David," yearning for an answer, longing for her daughter to be known. She does not tell the Lord what she needs. She simply sets before Him the reality of her daughter's oppression. The disciples are the ones who end up speaking. They see this woman as someone who needs to be sent away, maybe to remember where she belongs. She is a Gentile, after all, and is not a part of the promise of God.

Are there ways that we have felt belittled, like we do not deserve grace, or that our prayers are not worthy of God? Grace is a unique thing in that it is not earned. It is not inherited. It is completely and utterly undeserved mercy and empathy from God. There is a need for us, as disciples of Christ, to remember that everyone is a part of God's plan. Everything is covered by the overflowing abundance of God's grace. Let us not be like the disciples and push people away from a God who is calling everything into true harmony. Let us be like the Canaanite woman and bring everything before the feet of Christ in true submission with a heart of empathy as we love like the Serving King…
KD

The Sustainer

"Try to be a rainbow in someone's cloud." —Maya Angelou

He answered, "I was sent only to the lost sheep of the house of Israel." But she came and knelt before Him, saying, "Lord, help me." And He answered, "It is not right to take the children's bread and throw it to the dogs." She said, "Yes, Lord, yet even the dogs eat the crumbs that fall from their masters' table."

(Matthew 15: 24-27)

Jesus does not send the woman away. He speaks something that, potentially, the disciples believed to be true; He was there for them, not for her. Christ came for Israel, not the Gentiles. This is a common tension in Matthew, the Jewish and Gentile relationship. Jesus is Jewish, and He is the Lord, the Son of David. The Canaanite woman had stated this herself.

But her petition is sincere, and she falls before Him in submission, begging for help. Christ responded to her for the second time in this story, speaking matter-of-factly. This mother has been listening to Jesus' teaching though. She knows that this is a Savior that desires to make all things right. A Rabbi who feeds people with stories of the Kingdom of God but also with loaves of bread. Even though society may see her as a 'dog', she knows what matters most is that He is her Master.

This is a Master who has compassion, restores, and brings the Kingdom of God to the here and now. Christ came for Israel, but Christ is so much more than that. Christ came for the whole world! This woman understood this, unlike the disciples. God's plan does not fit within human reason or tradition. God works where mercy, grace, and life are needed. God is the sustainer of not just our hunger for food, but also healing. We may be satisfied if we ask and if we eat what God is giving to us.

Where are we hungry and needing sustenance? What do we need to ask for in our lives? Everyone is on a journey with Christ, but thanks be to God that we have a patient Master who feeds all our needs, no matter how the world may label us as unworthy. Such is the love of the Serving King...

KD

Redeemed

"If Christ has died for me, ungodly as I am, without strength as I am, then I cannot live in sin any longer, but must arouse myself to love and serve Him who has redeemed me." —Charles Spurgeon

Then Jesus answered her, "O woman, great is your faith! Be it done for you as you desire." And her daughter was healed instantly. (Matthew 15: 28)

The disciples and Jesus have uttered multiple phrases as to why this woman should go away. But she understands who this man is, Jesus Christ of all nations. She has prayed and petitioned for her daughter's healing as if it were her own infliction. She put aside social protocols and speaks to a Jew, asking for help. She even answers Jesus' quip with an answer that is faithful to the fact that Jesus is the Messiah and the Savior.

Listen to Jesus' words again: "O woman, great is your faith! Be it done for you as you desire." A good question here is, how often do our desires line up with God's redeeming nature? The world would look so drastically different if we truly prayed and brought before our Redeemer all the brokenness we witness in the world. This prayer starts with true empathy. Empathy is the taking on of another's feelings to the point that we will not be better till they are better. Prayer works through faith! Faith in a God who cares and has a plan. This plan may not line up with what we think will redeem the world, but we need to have faith that God's mission is the story we need to be a part of.

The woman is desiring God's mission for the world: for all things to be made new. For the redemption of Christ to rule over all, including her daughter's illness. How are we playing our role in God's mission for the world? It may be hard, it may hurt, but we are called to live radically different lives in this world. The Canaanite woman understands this when she prays to Jesus for healing. The disciples do not understand this radical shift as they call for her to be sent away. They should have been pleading alongside her.

How can we pray for healing in the world around us? Where are we called to be witnesses of the light that is possible even in the darkest of places? What places need the love of the Serving King most? Never hesitate to love like the Serving King....
KD

Healing On Demand...

Affliction brings out graces that cannot be seen in a time of health. It is the treading of the grapes that brings out the sweet juices of the vine; so it is affliction that draws forth submission, weans us from the world, and complete rest in God. Use afflictions while you have them. —Robert McShayne

They put them at His feet, and He cured them, so that the crowd was amazed when they saw the mute speaking, the maimed whole, the lame walking, and the blind seeing. And they praised the God of Israel. (Matthew 15:29-31)

This is one of the stories in the Bible that always gives me trouble. It is one of those stories where Jesus is recognized by all the healings He was doing. With stories like these, many people come to Christ today in search of healing for various maladies. We ask for healing, even plead, and some people proclaim that with enough faith we can expect healing. A simple equation that flows from a simple story like we have in this verse.

Here is the problem. In every city, there are people in cancer centers praying for a physical miracle. In neonatal units all over the world, parents pray for their children battling sicknesses that no child should ever have. Some of these prayers will be answered. Many others will not. This is the reality that we face – even believers with great faith.

Jesus was God, and it was important for Him to announce His presence to a world that knew only the power of Rome. The healings had a larger importance than just the physical lives of the people. With each healing, God was announcing that He was on Earth and was doing a new thing. If we notice the last part of the verse, the passage tells us that because of the healings, the crowds praised the God of Israel. The focus was God. This is the part we forget. If healing comes our way, the focus should be on the glory that of God. If we are not healed, we should still focus on the glory of God. We all want to be healed, but our faith is not dependent on whether that blessing comes our way. We know the reality of Christ, and have faith because of what happened in Matthew's time. If healing does not come, that is not a sign that we have been abandoned, but an opportunity to look around and minister to someone else who suffers with us. That may not be the answer we want, but the goal is not me, but what glory I can bring to God. Every Buddhist, Muslim, and Atheist prays to be healed. The truly Christian prayer is, "God, may my life bring honor and glory to You each and every day." Such is the way of those who love in the way of the Serving King...
DW

Hungry Sheep

"Jesus did not say—Make converts to your way of thinking, but look after My sheep, see that they get nourished in the knowledge of Me." —Oswald Chambers

And the disciples said to Him, "Where are we to get enough bread in such a desolate place to feed so great a crowd?　　　　　　(Matthew 15:33)

Jesus, the Master Shepherd, was not particularly successful in 'tending sheep', if success is measured by the response of the sheep. In fact, a close examination suggests the pre-resurrected Jesus was the victim of a mass 'sheep mutiny', even His own disciples, the 'sheep' of His inner pen, staying clear of Him in the final hours of His shepherding efforts. Hence, for the child trekking after the Serving King, there is little surprise in the fact the 'sheep' will require much 'tending' in the days that are to come. Hence, the repeated challenge of Jesus to 'tend my sheep'.

And rest assured, the sheep of Jesus have not changed much since He left. Tending them, especially in regard to making sure "...they get nourished in the knowledge of Me," will never be as simple as putting them out to pasture in the presence of the Church or His Word. They will not consume the 'knowledge of Me' as readily as you might hope.

You will be tempted to think, "If they were like me, thinking like I do, acting like I do, then I would find it much easier to love them, to tend them." Thus, you will set off to make converts to your way of 'thinking, being, and doing', teaching them your understanding of how this 'trek after the Serving King' should look. But alas, you will have forgotten a critical dimension of your trek after the Serving King; it is precisely that, your trek, custom-built for you by the Serving King. Your trek cannot be the trek of another, nor should it be.

But you can continually create opportunity for His sheep to find the pasture of His Word, for it is His Word which offers sheep the opportunity of nourishment. No shepherd can force the sheep to eat, but he can ensure his sheep always have access to nourishment. Love on in the way of the Serving King...

DM

The Inglorious Feeding

"After the first strike for God and for the right, God allowed Moses to be driven into blank discouragement, He sent him into the desert to feed sheep for forty years. At the end of that time, God appeared and told Moses to go and bring forth His people, and Moses said—'Who am I, that I should go?' In the beginning Moses realized that he was the man to deliver the people, but he had to be trained and disciplined by God first." —Oswald Chambers

And Jesus said to them, "How many loaves do you have?" They said, "Seven, and a few small fish." And directing the crowd to sit down on the ground, He took the seven loaves and the fish, and having given thanks He broke them and gave the to the disciples, and the disciples gave them to the crowds.

(Matthew 15:34-37)

Those called into that deepest of treks, a life of ministry, soon discover no life is fit for a 'life of ministry' without an extended period of "... feeding sheep in the desert." This 'extended' wilderness period, often for years on end, inglorious and mundane, seemingly to rotate around the inconsequential 'feeding of sheep', is ultimately not about the 'sheep' at all but, rather, the mandatory training period required of all those who will be used by God in significant ways. And feeding sheep often begins with the uncomfortable question, "How many loaves do you have?"

The Serving King is never shy about asking for your lunch. He often strips us of our resources for the sake of others. And you will wonder what He plans to do with so little, seven loaves and a few small fish. But little is always more than enough in the hands of the Serving King. Simply give Him what He asks for.

Many trekking after the Serving King, unbeknownst to them, are in the extended period of 'inglorious feeding', surrounded not only by 'sheep' wanting to be fed, but, additionally, 'sheep' unaware of the training they are inflicting upon those whom God is preparing. So you must be ever careful not to resent the 'sheep' whom God has chosen to strip you clean of every resource, even a 'few fish'. It is their chosen role, 'pots in the potter's hands' (Romans 9:21). These 'sheep' are part of God's inglorious wilderness for those soon to be deployed into significance by the Serving King. The 'inglorious feeding' is yet another critical step toward significance in loving in the ways of the Serving King...

DM

Satisfied For The Moment

"You entertain people who are satisfied. Hungry people can't be entertained - or people who are afraid. You can't entertain a man who has no food." —Bob Marley

And they all ate and were satisfied. And they took up seven baskets full of broken pieces left over. Those who ate were four thousand men, besides woman and children. And after sending away the crowds, He got into the boat and went to the region of Magadan. (Matthew 15:37-39)

Great teachers, especially the Serving King, understand the fundamentals of human nature. And one thing is certain, human beings love to eat, more than that, need to eat. Only the fool tries to teach a hungry person. Jesus is clearly no fool. Everyone eats. But eating is never the last page of the story; rather, it is just the beginning, the introduction, the appetizer for a grand and glorious tale.

Understand your need to eat, the hunger distracts you from the things that matter. And, if necessary, eat. Jesus understands. He often fed the multitudes. But realize there is a moment coming when Jesus will send you away, the time for eating over. There are more important things yet ahead for those who took the time to eat.

Still, it is in the time away from Him that hunger returns, yet again. The annoying cycle, consuming countless time and energy, repetitive in the most annoying ways. Surely life must be more than squelching the annoying pangs of hunger.

But it is the well-fed person who begins to ask the important questions in life, "Isn't life more than food and clothing? Isn't there more to life than the mundane?" And, of course, the answer is "yes." The quest of the well-fed person finally begins. It is they who are finally free to pursue the meaning of life, the reason for being here, life's ultimate purposes. It is they who are soon ready to return to Jesus, to seek more than food, to find life.

But today is not that day for most. They will remain in the cycle, relentlessly pursuing food that never satisfies beyond the moment. And so, He sends them away, back to the endless cycle, waiting for the 'hunger' that gives life to arrive. It is coming; especially for those whom He has fed. Patience. The Serving King patiently awaits. Patience is the way of those learning to love in the way of the Serving King…
DM

The Quest Continues…
This devotional has been divided into two parts, Vol. 1 and 2.
Volume 2 will appear in the Spring of 2019.